WILEY CPA EXAM REVIEW

Focus Notes

Financial Accounting and Reporting

F I F T H   E D I T I O N

D1552288

WILEY CPA EXAM REVIEW

Focus Notes

Financial Accounting and Reporting

F I F T H   E D I T I O N

Less Antman   Kevin Stevens, DBA, CPA

JOHN WILEY & SONS, INC.

Contents

Preface

This publication is a comprehensive, yet simplified study program. It provides a review of all the basic skills and concepts tested on the CPA exam, and teaches important strategies to take the exam faster and more accurately. This tool allows you to take control of the CPA exam.

This simplified and focused approach to studying for the CPA exam can be used:

- As a handy and convenient reference manual

- To solve exam questions

- To reinforce material being studied

Included is all of the information necessary to obtain a passing score on the CPA exam in a concise and easy-to-use format. Due to the wide variety of information covered on the exam, a number of techniques are included:

- Acronyms and mnemonics to help candidates learn and remember a variety of rules and checklists

- Formulas and equations that simplify complex calculations required on the exam

- Simplified outlines of key concepts without the details that encumber or distract from learning the essential elements

- Techniques that can be applied to problem solving or essay writing, such as preparing a multiple-step income statement, determining who will prevail in a legal conflict, or developing an audit program

- Pro forma statements, reports, and schedules that make it easy to prepare these items by simply filling in the blanks

- Proven techniques to help you become a smarter, sharper, and more accurate test taker

This publication may also be useful to university students enrolled in Intermediate, Advanced and Cost Accounting; Auditing, Business Law, and Federal Income Tax classes; Economics, and Finance classes.

Good Luck on the Exam,
Less Antman, CPA
Kevin Stevens, DBA, CPA

About the Authors

Less Antman, CPA, has been preparing individuals for the CPA exam since 1979. For many years, he taught CPA review classes on a full-time basis for various programs, including *Mark's CPA Review Course* and *Kaplan CPA Review*. He currently operates his own CPA review program in the state of California, under the name *Antman CPA Review,* located in Arcadia, California. He has taught more than 5,000 totally live CPA review classes, more than any other CPA review instructor in the United States, and his written materials have been used in several different instructor-based CPA review programs.

Kevin Stevens, DBA, CPA, is the director of the School of Accountancy and Management Information Systems at DePaul University. He is a full professor of accountancy and is a registered certified public accountant in Illinois. He has taught for many years in DePaul's CPA review program and at both the graduate and undergraduate levels. He holds a doctoral degree in business administration (accountancy) from the University of Kentucky, a master's in taxation from DePaul, a master's in accounting from the University of Illinois at Urbana and a bachelor's degree in Political Science from Loyola University, Chicago.

Objectives of Financial Reporting

Financial statements are designed to meet the objectives of financial reporting:

Balance Sheet	Direct Information	Financial Position
Statement of Earnings and Comprehensive Income	Direct Information	Entity Performance
Statement of Cash Flows	Direct Information	Entity Cash Flows
Financial Statements Taken As a Whole	Indirect Information	Management & Performance

Qualitative Characteristics of Accounting Information

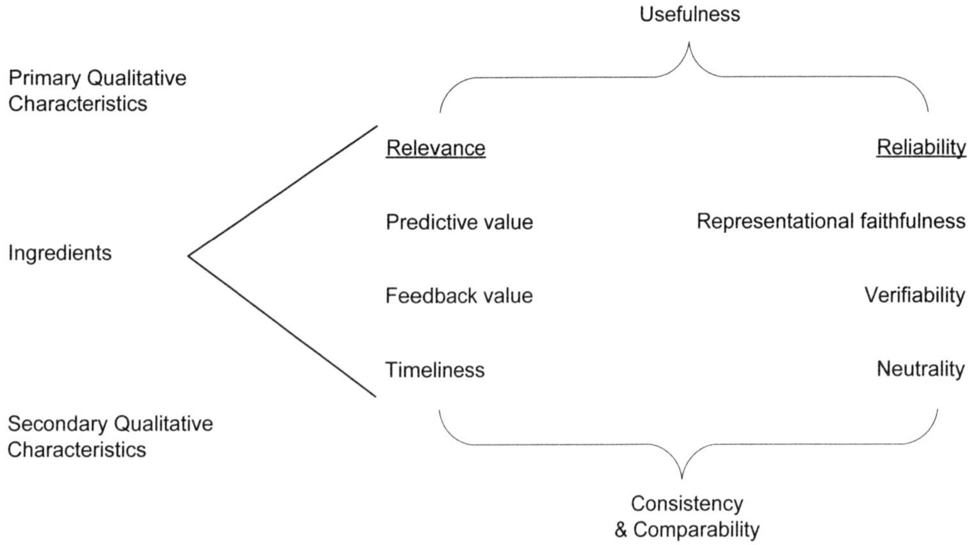

Usefulness

Primary Qualitative
Characteristics

Ingredients

Secondary Qualitative
Characteristics

<u>Relevance</u>

Predictive value

Feedback value

Timeliness

<u>Reliability</u>

Representational faithfulness

Verifiability

Neutrality

Consistency
& Comparability

Elements of Financial Statements

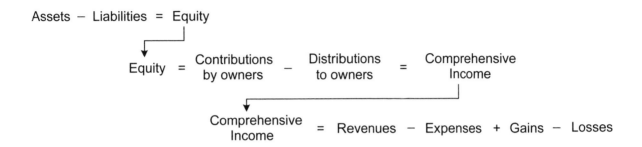

Assets − Liabilities = Equity

Equity = $\dfrac{\text{Contributions}}{\text{by owners}}$ − $\dfrac{\text{Distributions}}{\text{to owners}}$ = $\dfrac{\text{Comprehensive}}{\text{Income}}$

$\dfrac{\text{Comprehensive}}{\text{Income}}$ = Revenues − Expenses + Gains − Losses

Comprehensive Income = Net income ± Adjustments to stockholders' equity

Basic Rules & Concepts

Consistency

Realization

Conservatism

Recognition

Allocation

Matching

Full disclosure

*You'll get more credit (**CR**) if you **CRAM** your essays **FULL** of these rules and concepts*

Revenue Recognition

Accrual method   Collection reasonably assured
                        Degree of uncollectibility estimable

Installment sale   Collection not reasonably assured

Cost recovery   Collection not reasonably assured
                        No basis for determining whether or not collectible

Installment Sales Method

Installment receivable balance   Cash collections

× Gross profit percentage   × Gross profit percentage

= Deferred gross profit (balance sheet) = Realized gross profit (income statement)

Cost Recovery Method

All collections applied to cost before any profit or interest income is recognized

Converting from Cash Basis to Accrual Basis

Revenues

Cash (amount received)	xx	
Increase in accounts receivable (given)	xx	
Decrease in accounts receivable (given)		xx
Revenues (plug)		xx

Cost of Sales

Cost of sales (plug)	xx	
Increase in inventory (given)	xx	
Decrease in accounts payable (given)	xx	
Decrease in inventory (given)		xx
Increase in accounts payable (given)		xx
Cash (payments for merchandise)		xx

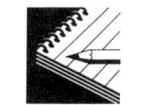

Expenses

Expense (plug)	xx	
Increase in prepaid expenses (given)	xx	
Decrease in accrued expenses (given)	xx	
Decrease in prepaid expenses (given)		xx
Increase in accrued expenses (given)		xx
Cash (amount paid for expense)		xx

Balance Sheet

Current Assets
Cash
Trading securities
Current securities available for sale
Accounts receivable
Inventories
Prepaid expenses
Current deferred tax asset

Long-Term Investments
Noncurrent securities available for sale
Securities held to maturity
Investments at cost or equity

Property, Plant, & Equipment
Intangibles
Other Assets
Deposits
Deferred charges
Noncurrent deferred tax asset

Current Liabilities
Short-term debt
Accounts payable
Accrued expenses
Current income taxes payable
Current deferred tax liability
Current portion of long-term debt
Unearned revenues

Long-Term Debt
Long-term notes payable
Bonds payable
Noncurrent deferred tax liability

Stockholders' Equity
Preferred stock
Common stock
Additional paid-in capital
Retained earnings
Accumulated other comprehensive income

Current Assets & Liabilities

Assets
- Economic resource
- Future benefit
- Control of company
- Past event or transaction

Liabilities
- Economic obligation
- Future sacrifice
- Beyond control of company
- Past event or transaction

Current Assets
- Converted into cash or used up
- Longer of:
    - One year
    - One accounting cycle

Current Liabilities
- Paid or settled
- Longer of:
    - One year
    - One accounting cycle

OR Requires use of current assets

Special Disclosures

Significant Accounting Policies

Inventory method

Depreciation method

Criteria for classifying investments

Method of accounting for long-term construction contracts

Related-Party Transactions

Exceptions:

    Salary

    Expense reimbursements

    Ordinary transactions

Reporting the Results of Operations

Preparing an Income Statement

Multiple step

    Revenues
-   Cost of sales
=   Gross profit
-   Operating expenses
      Selling expenses
      G & A expenses
=   Operating income
+   Other income
+   Gains
-   Other expenses
-   Losses
=   Income before taxes
-   Income tax expense
=   Income from continuing operations

Single step

    Revenues
+   Other income
+   Gains
=   Total revenues
-   Costs and expenses
      Cost of sales
      Selling expenses
      G & A expenses
      Other expenses
      Losses
      Income tax expense
=   Income from continuing operations

Computing Net Income

Income from continuing operations (either approach)

±   **D**iscontinued operations

±   **E**xtraordinary items

=   Net income

(Cumulative changes section was eliminated by SFAS 154)

Errors Affecting Income

Error (ending balance)	Current stmt	Prior stmt
Asset overstated	Overstated	No effect
Asset understated	Understated	No effect
Liability overstated	Understated	No effect
Liability understated	Overstated	No effect

Error (beginning balance – ending balance is correct)

	Current stmt	Prior stmt
Asset overstated	Understated	Overstated
Asset understated	Overstated	Understated
Liability overstated	Overstated	Understated
Liability understated	Understated	Overstated

Errors Affecting Income (continued)

Error (beginning balance – ending balance is not correct)

Asset overstated	No effect	Overstated
Asset understated	No effect	Understated
Liability overstated	No effect	Understated
Liability understated	No effect	Overstated

Extraordinary Items

Classification as extraordinary – 2 requirements (both must apply)
- Unusual in nature

- Infrequent of occurrence

One or neither applies – component of income from continuing operations

Extraordinary

Negative goodwill on consolidation resulted from purchase (always)
Acts of nature (usually)

Not Extraordinary

Gains or losses on sales of investments or prop, plant, & equip
Gains or losses due to changes in foreign currency exchange rates
Write-offs of inventory or receivables
Effects of major strikes or changes in value of investments

Change in Accounting Principle

Use **retrospective application** of new principle:

1) Calculate revised balance of asset or liability as of beginning of period as if new principle had always been in use.

2) Compare balance to amount reported under old method.

3) Multiply difference by 100% minus tax rate.

4) Result is treated on books as prior period adjustment to beginning retained earnings.

5) All previous periods being presented in comparative statements restated to new principle.

6) Beginning balance of earliest presented statement of retained earnings adjusted for all effects going back before that date.

Change in Accounting Principle (continued)

Journal entry:

Asset or liability	xxx	
Retained earnings		xxx
Current or deferred tax liability (asset)		xxx

Or

Retained earnings	xxx	
Current or deferred tax liability (asset)	xxx	
Asset or liability		xxx

Special Changes

Changes in accounting principle are handled using the **prospective** method under limited circumstances. No calculation is made of prior period effects and the new principle is simply applied starting at the beginning of the current year when the following changes in principle occur:

- Changes in the method of depreciation, amortization, or depletion
- Changes whose effect on prior periods is impractical to determine (e.g. changes to LIFO when records don't allow computation of earlier LIFO cost bases)

(Note: the method of handling changes in accounting principle described here under SFAS 154 replaces earlier approaches, which applied the **cumulative method** to most changes in accounting principle. SFAS 154 abolished the use of the cumulative method.)

Change in Estimate

- No retrospective application
- Change applied as of beginning of current period
- Applied in current and future periods

Error Corrections

Applies to:

- Change from unacceptable principle to acceptable principle
- Errors in prior period financial statements

When error occurred:

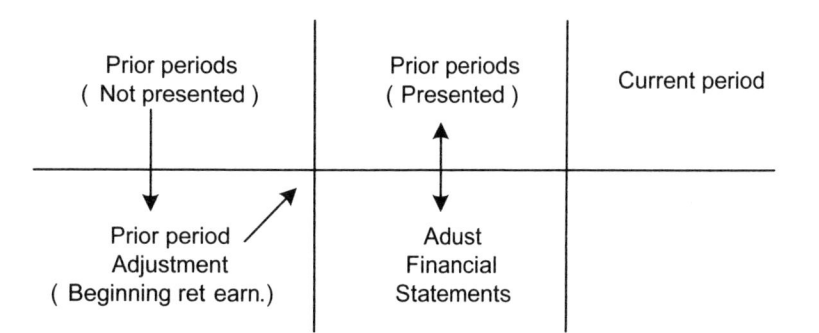

Prior periods (Not presented)	Prior periods (Presented)	Current period
Prior period Adjustment (Beginning ret earn.)	Adust Financial Statements	

Discontinued Operations

When components of a business are disposed of, their results are reported in discontinued operations:

- Component – An asset group whose activities can be distinguished from the remainder of the entity both operationally and for financial reporting purposes.
- Disposal – Either the assets have already been disposed of or they are being held for sale and the entity is actively searching for a buyer and believes a sale is probable at a price that can be reasonably estimated.

All activities related to the component are reported in discontinued operations, including those occurring prior to the commitment to dispose and in prior periods being presented for comparative purposes.

Reporting Discontinued Operations

Lower section of the income statement:

- After income from continuing operations
- Before extraordinary items

Reported amount each year includes all activities related to the component from operations as well as gains and losses on disposal, net of income tax effects

- Expected gains and losses from operations in future periods are not reported until the future period in which they occur.

Impairment loss is included in the current period when the fair market value of the component is believed to be lower than carrying amount based on the anticipated sales price of the component in future period

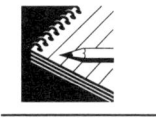

Reporting Comprehensive Income

Statement of Comprehensive Income required as one of financial statements

- May be part of Income statement
- May be separate statement
- Begin with net income
- Add or subtract items of other comprehensive income

Other comprehensive income includes:

- Current year's unrealized gains or losses on securities available for sale

- Current year's foreign currency translation adjustments

- Current year's unrealized gains or losses resulting from changes in market values of certain derivatives being used as cash flow hedges

Accounting for Changing Prices

Accounting at Current Cost

Assets & liabilities reported at current amounts

Income statement items adjusted to current amounts

- Inventory reported at replacement cost
- Cost of sales = Number of units sold × Average current cost of units during period
- Differences in inventory & cost of sales treated as holding gains or losses
- Depreciation & amortization – Computed using same method & life based on current cost

Accounting for Changes in Price Level

Purchasing power gains & losses relate only to **monetary** items

- Monetary assets – money or claim to receive money such as cash & net receivables
- Monetary liabilities – obligations to pay specific amounts of money

Company may be monetary creditor or debtor

- Monetary creditor – monetary assets > monetary liabilities
- Monetary debtor – monetary liabilities > monetary assets

In periods of rising prices

- Monetary creditor will experience purchasing power loss
- Monetary debtor will experience purchasing power gain

Inventories

Goods In Transit

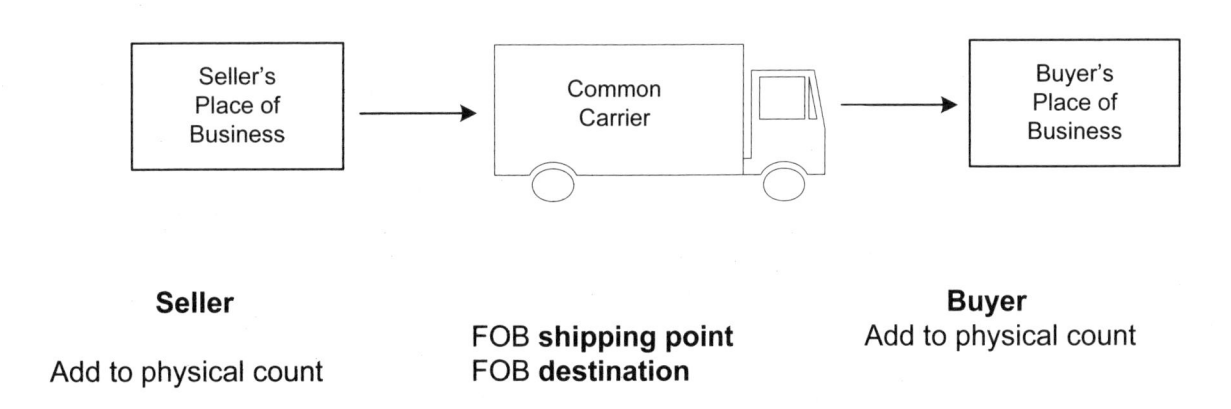

| Seller's Place of Business | Common Carrier | Buyer's Place of Business |

Seller

Add to physical count

FOB **shipping point**
FOB **destination**

Buyer
Add to physical count

Inventory Cost

Purchase price
+ Freight in
+ Costs incurred in preparing for sale
= Inventory cost

Goods on Consignment

Consignee — Exclude from physical count
Consignor — Add to physical count (at cost)

Cost of goods on consignment =

Inventory cost
+ Cost of shipping to consignee

Abnormal costs expensed in current period instead of being included in inventory:

- Idle facility expense
- Wasted materials in production
- Double freight when items returned and redelivered

Cost of Goods Sold

Beginning inventory
<u>+　Net purchases</u>
=　Cost of goods available for sale
<u>–　Ending inventory</u>
=　Cost of goods sold

Inventory Errors

	Beg. RE	COGS	Gross Profit	End RE
Beginning – overstated	Over	Over	Under	No effect
Beginning – understated	Under	Under	Over	No effect
Ending – overstated	No effect	Under	Over	Over
Ending – understated	No effect	Over	Under	Under

Periodic Versus Perpetual

	Periodic	_Perpetual_

Buy merchandise:	Purchases
	   Accounts payable
		Inventory
		   Accounts payable

Sell merchandise	Accounts receivable
	   Sales
		Accounts receivable
		   Sales
		Cost of goods sold
		   Inventory

Record cost of
 goods sold
	Ending inventory (count)
	Cost of goods sold (plug)
	   Purchases (net amount)
	   Beginning inventory (balance)	

FIFO – Same under either method

LIFO – Different amounts for periodic and perpetual

Average – Different amounts for periodic and perpetual
       Periodic – Weighted-average

Inventory Valuation Methods

	Ending Inventory	Cost of Goods Sold	Gross Profit
Periods of rising prices:			
FIFO	Highest	Lowest	Highest
LIFO	Lowest	Highest	Lowest
Periods of falling prices:			
FIFO	Lowest	Highest	Lowest
LIFO	Highest	Lowest	Highest

Applying LIFO

Step 1 – Determine ending quantity

Step 2 – Compare to previous period's ending quantity

Step 3 – Increases – Add new layer

Step 4 – Small decreases (less than most recent layer) – Reduce most recent layer

Step 5 – Large decreases (more than most recent layer) – Eliminate most recent layer or layers and decrease next most recent layer

Step 6 – Apply appropriate unit price to each layer

For each layer:

$$\frac{\text{Inventory}}{\text{Quantity}} \times \frac{\text{Price}}{\text{per unit}} = \frac{\text{Inventory}}{\text{Value}}$$

Application of LIFO

Information given:

	Ending Quantity	Price per unit
Year 1	10,000 units	$5.00
Year 2	12,000 units	$5.50
Year 3	15,000 units	$6.00
Year 4	13,500 units	$6.50
Year 5	11,200 units	$7.00
Year 6	13,200 units	$7.50

Information applied:

Year 1:

Base layer	10,000 units	$5.00	$50,000
Total	**10,000 units**		**$50,000**

Application of LIFO (continued)

Year 2:

Year 2 layer	2,000 units	$5.50	$11,000
Base layer	10,000 units	$5.00	$50,000
Total	**12,000 units**		**$61,000**

Year 3:

Year 3 layer	3,000 units	$6.00	$18,000
Year 2 layer	2,000 units	$5.50	$11,000
Base layer	10,000 units	$5.00	$50,000
Total	**15,000 units**		**$79,000**

Application of LIFO (continued)

Year 4:

Year 3 layer	1,500 units	$6.00	$9,000
Year 2 layer	2,000 units	$5.50	$11,000
Base layer	10,000 units	$5.00	$50,000
Total	**13,500 units**		**$70,000**

Year 5:

Year 2 layer	1,200 units	$5.50	$6,600
Base layer	10,000 units	$5.00	$50,000
Total	**11,200 units**		**$56,600**

Application of LIFO (continued)

Year 6:

Year 3 layer	2,000 units	$7.50	$15,000
Year 2 layer	1,200 units	$5.50	$6,600
Base layer	10,000 units	$5.00	$50,000
Total	**13,200 units**		**$71,600**

Dollar-Value LIFO

Less cumbersome than LIFO for inventory consisting of many items

Combines inventory into pools

Increases in some items within a pool offset decreases in others

Applying Dollar-Value LIFO

Step 1 – Determine ending inventory at current year's prices

Step 2 – Divide by current price level index to convert to base year prices

Step 3 – Compare to previous period's ending inventory at base year prices

Step 4 – Increases – Add new layer at base year prices

Step 5 – Small decreases (less than most recent layer) – Reduce most recent layer

Step 6 – Large decreases (more than most recent layer) – Eliminate most recent layer or layers
and decrease next most recent layer

Step 7 – Apply appropriate unit price to each layer

For each layer:

$$\text{Inventory amount at base year prices} \times \text{Price index} = \text{Inventory amount Dollar-Value LIFO}$$

Application of Dollar-Value LIFO

Information given:

	Ending Inventory at Current Prices	Price level index
Year 1	$200,000	100
Year 2	243,800	106
Year 3	275,000	110
Year 4	255,200	116

Information applied:

Year 1	*Base year prices*	*Index*	*Dollar-Value LIFO*
Base layer	$200,000	100	$200,000
Total	$200,000		$200,000

Application of Dollar-Value LIFO (continued)

Year 2:

$243,800 ÷ 1.06 = $230,000 (at base year prices)

	Base year prices	*Index*	*Dollar-Value LIFO*
Year 2 layer	$30,000	106	$31,800
Base layer	$200,000	100	$200,000
Total	$230,000		$231,800

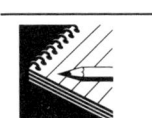

Application of Dollar-Value LIFO (continued)

Year 3:

$275,000 ÷ 1.10 = $250,000 (at base year prices)

	Base year prices	*Index*	*Dollar-Value LIFO*
Year 3 layer	$20,000	110	$22,000
Year 2 layer	$30,000	106	$31,800
Base layer	$200,000	100	$200,000
Total	$250,000		$253,800

Application of Dollar-Value LIFO (continued)

Year 4:

$255,200 ÷ 1.16 = $220,000 (at base year prices)

	Base year prices	Index	Dollar-Value LIFO
Year 2 layer	$20,000	106	$21,200
Base layer	$200,000	100	$200,000
Total	$220,000		$221,200

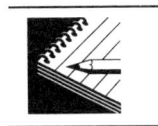

Dollar-Value LIFO – Calculating a Price Level Index

Simplified LIFO – Company uses a published index

Double Extension Method – Cumulative index

Compare current year to base year

$$\frac{\text{Ending inventory at current year's prices}}{\text{Ending inventory at base year prices}}$$

Link Chain Method – Annual index

Compare current year to previous year

$$\frac{\text{Ending inventory at current year's prices}}{\text{Ending inventory at previous year's prices}}$$

Lower of Cost or Market

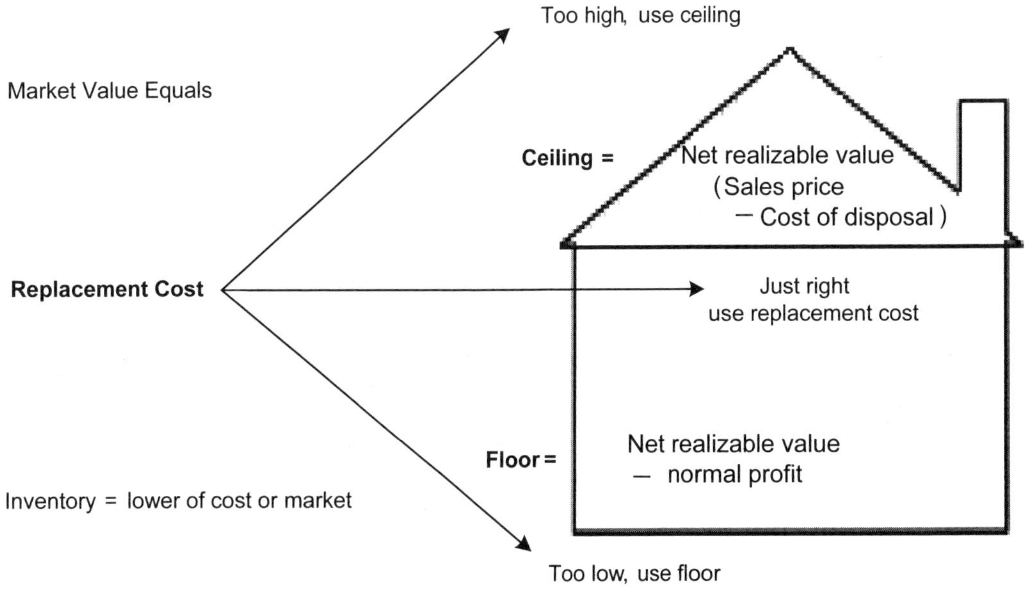

Too high, use ceiling

Market Value Equals

Ceiling = Net realizable value
(Sales price
— Cost of disposal)

Replacement Cost → Just right
use replacement cost

Floor = Net realizable value
— normal profit

Inventory = lower of cost or market

Too low, use floor

Gross Profit Method for Estimating Inventory

If gross profit is **percentage of sales**:

    Sales   100%

    − Cost of sales

    = Gross profit

If gross profit is **percentage of cost**:

    Sales

    − Cost of sales   100%

    = Gross profit

To find cost of sales

Sales × (100% − Gross profit %)

Sales ÷ (100% + Gross profit%)

Beginning inventory

+   Net purchases

=   Cost of goods available

−   Cost of sales

=   Ending inventory

Conventional Retail (Lower of Cost or Market)

	Cost	Retail		C/R%
Beginning inventory	xx	xx		
+ Net purchases	xx	xx		
+ Freight in	xx			
+ Net markups		xx		
= Cost of goods available for sale	xx	xx		Cost / Retail
− Sales (retail)			xx	
Net markdowns			xx	
Employee discounts			xx	
Spoilage (retail)		(xx)	xx	
= Ending inventory at retail		xx		
× Cost to retail percentage		x%		
= Ending inventory at approximate lower of cost or market		xx		

Long-Term Construction Contracts

Percentage of Completion

Use when:

- Estimates of costs are reasonably dependable
- Estimates of progress toward completion

Reporting profit

- Recognized proportionately during contract
- Added to construction in process

Balance sheet amount

- Current asset – excess of costs and estimated profits over billings
- Current liability – excess of billings over costs and estimated profits

Long-Term Construction Contracts (Continued)

Calculating profit:

Step 1 – Total profit

Contract price		xxx
Total estimated cost		
Cost incurred to date (**1**)	xxx	
Estimated cost to complete	+ xxx	
Total estimated cost (**2**)		– xxx
Total estimated profit (**3**)		= xxx

Step 2 – % of completion (Cost to cost method)

    Costs incurred to date (**1**) ÷ Total estimated cost (**2**) = % of completion (**4**)

Step 3 – Profit to date

    % of completion (**4**) × Total estimated profit (**3**) = Estimated profit to date (**5**)

Step 4 – Current period's profit

    Estimated profit to date (**5**) – Profit previously recognized = Current period's profit

Long-Term Construction Contracts (continued)

Recognizing Losses

When loss expected:

Estimated loss	xxx
+ Profit recognized to date	<u>xxx</u>
= Amount of loss to recognize	<u>xxx</u>

Completed Contract

Income statement amount

- Profit recognized in period of completion
- Loss recognized in earliest period estimable

Balance sheet amount

- Current assets – excess of costs over billings
- Current liabilities – excess of billings over costs

Property, Plant, & Equipment

General Rule:

Capitalized amount = Cost of asset + Costs incurred in preparing it for its intended use

    Cost of asset = FMV of asset received **or**

        Cash paid + FMV of assets given

Gifts:

      Asset (FMV) xx

           Income   xx

Other capitalized costs for assets acquired by gift or purchase:

      Shipping

      Insurance during shipping

      Installation

      Testing

Land and Building

Total cost:

Purchase price

Delinquent taxes assumed

Legal fees

Title insurance

Allocation to land and building – **Relative Fair Market Value Method**

FMV of land

+ FMV of building

= Total FMV

Land = FMV of land ÷ Total FMV × Total Cost

Building = FMV of building ÷ Total FMV × Total Cost

Capitalization of Interest

Capitalize on:

    Assets constructed for company's use

    Assets manufactured for resale resulting from special order

Do not capitalize on:

    Inventory manufactured in the ordinary course of business

Interest capitalized:

    Interest on debt incurred for construction of asset

    Interest on other debt that could be avoided by repayment of debt

Computed on:

    Weighted-average accumulated expenditures

Costs Incurred After Acquisition

Capitalize if:

- **Bigger** – the cost makes the asset bigger, such as an addition to a building
- **Better** – the cost makes the asset better, such as an improvement that makes an asset perform more efficiently
- **Longer** – the cost makes the asset last longer, it extends the useful life

Do not capitalize:

Repairs and maintenance

Depreciation and Depletion

Basic Terms:

Straight-line rate = 100% ÷ Useful life (in years)

Book value = Cost − Accumulated depreciation

Depreciable basis = Cost − Salvage value

Selection of Method:

Use **straight-line** when benefit from asset is uniform over life

Use **accelerated** when:

Asset more productive in earlier years

Costs of maintenance increase in later years

Risk of obsolescence is high

Use **units-of-production** when usefulness decreases with use

Straight-Line

Annual depreciation =

Depreciable basis

  × Straight-line rate

Partial year =

  Annual depreciation

  × Portion of year

Double-Declining Balance

Annual depreciation =

Book value

  × Straight-line rate

  × 2

Partial year =

  Book value

  × Straight-line rate

  × 2

  × Portion of year

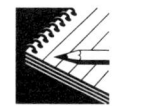

Sum-of-the-Years'-Digits

Annual depreciation =

Depreciable basis

× Fraction	1st Year	2nd Year	3rd Year
Numerator =	n	$n-1$	$n-2$
Denominator =	$n(n+1) \div 2$	$n(n+1) \div 2$	$n(n+1) \div 2$

Partial year:

1st year = 1st year's depreciation × portion of year

2nd year = Remainder of 1st year's depreciation
+ 2nd year's depreciation × portion of year

3rd year = Remainder of 2nd year's depreciation
+ 3rd year's depreciation × portion of year

Units-of-Production

Depreciation rate = **Depreciable basis** ÷ Total estimated units to be produced (hours)

Annual depreciation =

    Depreciation rate

    × Number of units produced (hours used)

Group or Composite

Based on straight-line

Gains or losses not recognized on disposal

Cash (proceeds)	xx	
Accumulated depreciation (plug)	xx	
Asset (original cost)		xx

Impairment

Occurs if undiscounted future cash flow less than asset carrying amount from events such as:

A decrease in the market value of the asset

An adverse action or assessment by a regulator

An operating or cash flow loss associated with a revenue producing asset

When an impairment loss occurs:

Asset is written down to fair market value (or discounted net cash flow):

Loss due to impairment	xx	
Accumulated depreciation		xx

Note that test for impairment (future cash flow) is different from write-down amount (net realizable value)

Application of Impairment Rules

Example 1:

Asset carrying value – $1,000,000
Undiscounted future cash flow expected from asset – $900,000
Fair market value of asset – $600,000

Impairment exists – $900,000 expected cash flow less than $1,000,000 carrying amount

Write asset down by $400,000 ($1,000,000 reduced to $600,000)

Example 2:

Asset carrying value – $800,000
Undiscounted future cash flow expected from asset – $900,000
Fair market value of asset – $600,000

No impairment adjustment – $900,000 expected cash flow exceeds $800,000 carrying amount

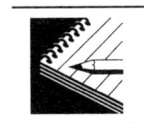

Disposal of Property, Plant, & Equipment

Cash (proceeds)	xx	
Accumulated depreciation (balance)	xx	
Loss on disposal (plug)	xx	
Gain on disposal (plug)		xx
Asset (original cost)		xx

A disposal in **involuntary conversion** is recorded in the same manner as a sale

Nonmonetary Exchanges

Cash (amount received)		
Asset – New (FMV)	xx	
Accumulated depreciation (balance on old asset)	xx	
Loss on disposal (plug)		
Cash (amount paid)		
Gain on disposal (plug)		xx
Asset – Old (Original cost)		xx

FMV

Use fair value of asset received **or**

Fair value of asset given

+   Cash paid

–   Cash received

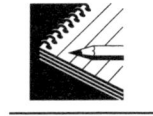

Nonmonetary Exchanges (continued)

Exception

Applies to exchanges when:

- FMV is not determinable
- Exchange is only to facilitate subsequent sales to customers (e.g. ownership of inventory in one city is swapped for similar inventory in another to facilitate prompt delivery to customer in distant city)
- Transaction lacks commercial substance (risk, timing, and amount of future cash flows will not significantly change as a result of the transaction).

Loss – FMV of asset given < Carrying value of asset given

Cash (amount received)	xx	
Asset – New (FMV)	xx	
Loss on disposal (plug)	xx	
Cash (amount paid)		xx
Asset – Old (carrying value)		xx

Nonmonetary Exchanges (continued)

Gain – FMV of asset given > Carrying value of asset given

Gain recognized only when cash received

FMV of asset given
   − Carrying value of asset given
   = Total gain
   × Percentage
   = Gain recognized

$$\frac{\text{Cash received}}{\text{Total proceeds (Cash + FMV of asset received)}}$$

Cash (amount received)	xx	
Asset—New (plug)	xx	
Gain on disposal (computed amount)		xx
Asset—Old (carrying value)		xx

Nonmonetary Exchanges (continued)

No gain recognized when cash paid or no cash involved

Asset – New (plug)	XX	
Accumulated depreciation (balance on old asset)	XX	
Cash (amount paid)		XX
Asset – Old (original cost)		XX

Intangibles

General Characteristics

Lack physical substance

Uncertain benefit period

Associated with legal rights

Initial Accounting

Capitalize costs of purchasing intangibles

Expense costs of developing intangibles internally

Capitalize costs of preparing for use
   Legal fees
   Registration fees

Amortization

Straight-line amortization

Amortized over **shorter** of:

    Legal life

    Useful life

Units of sales amortization used if greater than straight-line

Tested for impairment when events suggest undiscounted future cash flow will be less than carrying value of intangible – written down to fair market value

Intangibles with no clear legal or useful life (trademarks, perpetual franchises) tested annually for impairment and written down whenever fair market value is less than carrying value

Goodwill

Acquisition

Must be part of (purchase) business combination

Excess of purchase price over fair value of underlying net assets

Internal costs

May incur development or maintenance costs

All costs are expensed

Amortization

No amortization recorded

Test annually for impairment of value

Goodwill written down whenever fair market value less than carrying value

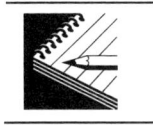

Leasehold Improvements

Amortize over shorter of:

- Useful life
- Remaining term of lease

Patents

Legal costs of defending a patent

- Successful – capitalize legal costs as addition to carrying value of patent
- Unsuccessful – recognize legal costs as expense and consider writing down patent

Research and Development (R & D)

Research – aimed at discovery of new knowledge

New product or process

Improvement to existing product or process

Development – converting new knowledge into plan or design

R & D assets:

Used for general R & D activities

Capitalize

Depreciate

Charge to R & D expense

Used for specific project

Charge to R & D expense

Startup Costs

Costs associated with startup of organization should be immediately expensed

Franchises

Initial fee – generally capitalized and amortized

Subsequent payments – generally recognized as expense in period incurred

Software

Expense – cost up to technological feasibility

Capitalize and amortize – costs from technological feasibility to start of production

- Coding and testing
- Production of masters

Charge to inventory – costs incurred during production

Software (continued)

Time line:

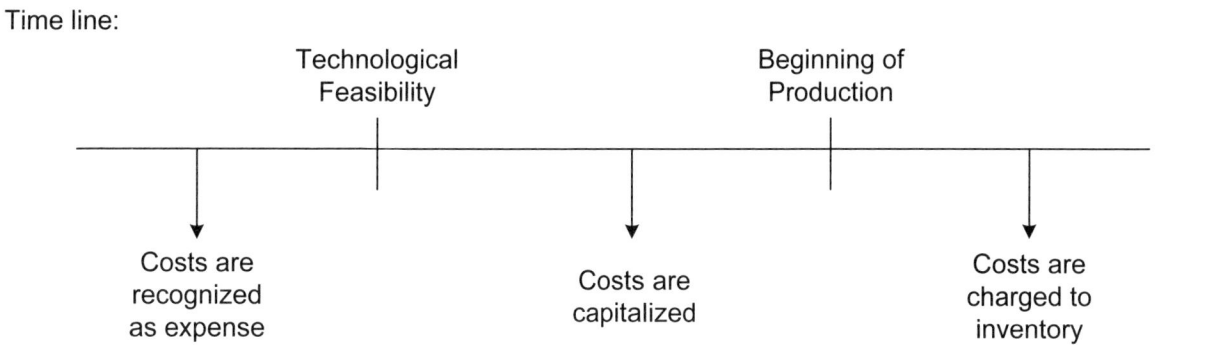

Software (continued)

Amortization of capitalized software costs – larger of:

Straight-line	or	**Ratio**
$$\dfrac{\text{Carrying value}}{\text{Remaining useful life}}$$		$$\dfrac{\text{Current revenues} \times \text{Carrying value}}{\text{Estimated remaining revenues}}$$
(Current period + future periods)		(Current revenues + future revenues)

Additional amortization:

Carrying value (after amortization) > Net realizable value (based on future revenues)

Excess is additional amortization

Bank Reconciliation

Bank balance
+ Deposits in transit
− Outstanding checks
± Errors made by bank
= Corrected balance

Book balance
Amounts collected by bank +
Unrecorded bank charges −
Errors made when recording transactions ±
Corrected balance =

Must be equal

Accounts Receivable

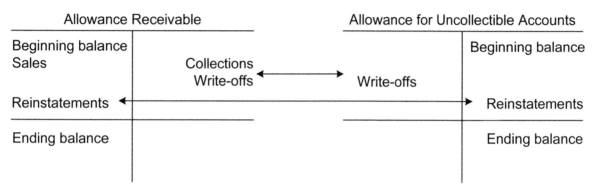

Allowance Receivable

Beginning balance	
Sales	Collections
	Write-offs
Reinstatements	
Ending balance	

Allowance for Uncollectible Accounts

	Beginning balance
Write-offs	
	Reinstatements
	Ending balance

Net realizable value = Accounts receivable – Allowance for Uncollectible Accounts

Uncollectible Accounts

Income Statement Approach

Credit sales
× % uncollectible (given)
= Bad debt expense

Balance Sheet Approach

Accounts receivable balance
× Portion uncollectible
= Ending balance in allowance

Allowance for Uncollectible Accounts

Accounts written off	Beginning balance Bad debt expense Reinstatements
	Ending balance

Calculate expense and plug balance **or** calculate balance and plug expense

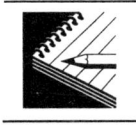

Uncollectible Accounts

Allowance Methods - GAAP

Matching concept – Bad debt expense in period of sale

Measurement concept – Accounts receivable at net realizable value

Direct Write-off Method - Non-GAAP

Violates matching concept – Bad debt expense when account written off

Violates measurement concept – Accounts receivable overstated at gross amount

Notes Received for Cash

Calculating Payment

Principal amount ÷ Present value factor = Payment amount

> Present value factor for annuity based on number of payments and interest rate

Allocating Payments

Payment amount − Interest = Principal reduction

Calculating Interest

Beginning balance
- × Interest rate
- × Period up to payment
- = Interest up to payment

Balance after principal reduction
- × Interest rate
- × Period up to payment to year-end
- = Interest for remainder of year

Add together for total interest

Notes Received for Goods or Services

Note Balance

Short-term: Amount = Face value

Long-term: Amount =

    Fair value of goods or services

    Present value of payments if fair value not known

Journal entry:

Note receivable - Face amount (given)   xxx

      Revenue - Calculated amount   xxx

      Discount on note receivable (plug)   xxx

Notes Received for Goods or Services

Interest Income

Face amount of note
- Unamortized discount
= Carrying value of note
× Interest rate
= Interest income

Journal entry:

Discount on note receivable	xxx
Interest income	xxx

Financing Receivables - Discounting

Proceeds From Discounting

Face amount

+   Interest income (Face × Interest rate × Term)

=   Maturity value

−   Discount (Maturity value × Discount rate × Remaining term)

=   Proceeds

Financing Receivables

Financing Without Recourse

Treated as sale – referred to as factoring

Cash	xxx	
Loss on sale (plug)	xxx	
Accounts receivable (balance)		xxx

Financing With Recourse

Treated as loan – may be referred to as assignment

Cash - Proceeds (given)	xxx	
Note payable secured by receivables		xxx
Accounts receivable assigned	xxx	
Accounts receivable (balance)		xxx

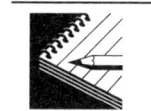

Financial Statement Analysis

Ratios Involving Current Assets & Liabilities

Working capital = current assets – current liabilities

Current ratio = current assets ÷ current liabilities

Quick ratio = quick assets ÷ current liabilities

Quick assets – current assets readily convertible into cash

- Cash

- Accounts receivable

- Investments in trading securities

Ratios Involving Receivables

Accounts receivable turnover = Credit sales ÷ Average accounts receivable

Days to collect accounts receivable = 365 ÷ Accounts receivable turnover

or

Days to collect accounts receivable = Average accounts receivable ÷ Average sales/day

Average sales/day = Credit sales ÷ 365

Ratios Involving Inventories

Inventory turnover = Cost of sales ÷ Average inventory

Days sales in inventory = 365 ÷ Inventory turnover

or

Days sales in inventory = Average inventory ÷ Average inventory sold/day

Average inventory sold/day = Cost of sales ÷ 365

Other Ratios

Operating cycle = Days to collect accounts receivable + Days sales in inventory

Debt to total assets = Total debt ÷ Total assets

Debt to equity = Total debt ÷ Total stockholders' equity

Return on assets = Net income ÷ Average total assets

Accounts Payable

Purchase shipment terms	Payable already recorded	Payable not already recorded
Shipping point	No adjustment	Adjust – add
Destination	Adjust – deduct	No adjustment

Contingencies

Loss Contingencies

Probable – Accrue & disclose

- Not estimable – Disclose only
- Estimable within range – Accrue minimum of range

Reasonably possible – Disclose only

Remote – Neither accrued nor disclosed

Gain Contingencies

Never accrue (until realization occurs or is assured beyond reasonable doubt)

May disclose

Estimated & Accrued Amounts

Money 1st – Goods or services 2nd

- Expenses – prepaid
- Revenues – unearned

Goods or services 1st – Money 2nd

- Expenses – accrued
- Revenues – receivable

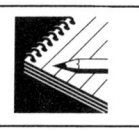

Revenue Items

Calculate amount earned or amount collected

1) Determine changes in accrual items:

	Debit	Credit
Revenue receivable	Increase	Decrease
Unearned revenue	Decrease	Increase

2) Prepare journal entry

Cash	xxx		
Revenue receivable	xxx	or	xxx
Unearned revenue	xxx	or	xxx
Revenues			xxx

3) If amount collected is given, that is the debit to cash and the amount required to balance the entry is the amount earned. If the amount earned is given, that is the credit to revenues and the amount required to balance the entry is the amount collected

Expense Items

Calculate amount incurred or amount paid

1) Determine changes in accrual items:

	Debit	_Credit_
Prepaid expense	Increase	Decrease
Accrued expense	Decrease	Increase

2) Prepare journal entry

Expense	xxx	
Prepaid expense	xxx or	xxx
Accrued expense	xxx or	xxx
Cash		xxx

3) If amount paid is given, that is the credit to cash and the amount required to balance the entry is the amount incurred. If the amount incurred is given, that is the debit to expense and the amount required to balance the entry is the amount paid

---

Insurance

Prepaid insurance (end of year)

Total premiums paid × Months remaining / Total # of months

Insurance expense

Prepaid insurance (beginning) + Premiums paid – Prepaid insurance (ending)

Royalties

Royalty income for current year

1st payment – includes royalties earned in latter part of previous period early in current period
- Include payment
- Deduct royalties from previous period

2nd payment – received for royalties earned during current period

- Include entire payment

Additional royalties

- Add royalties earned for latter part of current period

Service Contract

Service contract revenues – fees received uniformly during period

    Fees received

    × % earned in 1st period

    × 50%

Deferred service contract revenues

    Fees received

    −   service contract revenues

Coupons

Discounts on merchandise

Number of coupons not expired

× % expected to be redeemed

× Cost per coupon (face + service fee)

− Amount already paid

= Liability

Premiums (Prizes)

Number of units sold

× % expected to be redeemed

÷ number required per prize

− Prizes already sent

× Cost per prize

= Liability

Warranties

Warranty expense

    Sales
× % of warranty costs
= Expense for period

Warranty liability

Estimated warranty liability

Payments	Beg. bal.
	Expense
	End bal.

Compensated Absences

Four conditions:

- Past services of employees
- Amounts vest or accumulate
- Probable
- Estimable

When all conditions met:

	Vest	*Accumulate*
Vacation pay	Must accrue	Must accrue
Sick pay	Must accrue	May accrue

Miscellaneous Liabilities

Refinancing Liabilities

To exclude from current liabilities – 2 requirements:

- Company intends to refinance on a long-term basis
- Company can demonstrate ability to refinance

The ability to refinance can be demonstrated in either of 2 ways:

- Refinance on long-term basis after balance sheet date but before issuance

- Enter into firm agreement with lender having ability to provide long-term financing

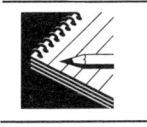

Accounting for Leases

Lessee Reporting

Rights & risks of ownership transfer from lessor to lessee?

Yes

No

Capital lease

Operating lease

Transfer of rights & risks of ownership – At least 1 of 4 criteria

Actual transfer

- Title transfers to lessee by end of term
- Lease contains bargain purchase option

Transfer in substance

- Lease term $\geq$ 75% of useful life
- Present value of min lease payments $\geq$ 90% of fair market value

To calculate present value – lessee uses lower of:

- Incremental borrowing rate
- Rate implicit in lease (if known)

Capital Leases

Inception of lease

Journal entry to record lease:

Leased asset	xxx	
Lease obligation		xxx

Amount of asset & liability = PV of minimum lease payments:

- Payments beginning at inception result in annuity due
- Payments beginning at end of first year result in ordinary annuity
- Payments include bargain purchase option or guaranteed residual value (lump sum at end of lease)

Lease payments

Payment at inception:

Lease obligation	xxx	
Cash		xxx

Subsequent payments:

Interest expense	xxx	
Lease obligation	xxx	
Cash		xxx

Interest amount:

Balance in lease obligation

×   Interest rate (used to calculate PV)

×   Time since last payment (usually 1 year)

=   Interest amount

Periodic Expenses - Depreciation

Actual transfer (1 of first 2 criteria)

- Life = useful life of property
- Salvage value taken into consideration

Transfer in substance (1 of latter 2 criteria)

- Life = shorter of useful life or lease term
- No salvage value

Periodic Expenses - Executory costs

Consist of insurance, maintenance, & taxes

Recognized as expense when incurred

Balance Sheet Presentation

Leased asset

- Reported as P, P, & E
- Reported net of accumulated depreciation

Lease obligation

- Current liability = Principal payments due in subsequent period
- Noncurrent liability = Remainder

Disclosures

- Amount of assets recorded under capital leases
- Minimum lease payments for each of next 5 years and in aggregate
- Description of leasing activities

Lessor Reporting

Rights & risks of ownership transfer from lessor to lessee?

Yes

No

Additional criteria

Operating lease

Transfer of rights & risks of ownership – At least 1 of 4 criteria

- Same criteria as lessee
- To calculate present value – lessor uses rate implicit in lease

Additional Criteria

- Collectibility of lease payments reasonably predictable
- No significant uncertainties as to costs to be incurred in connection with lease

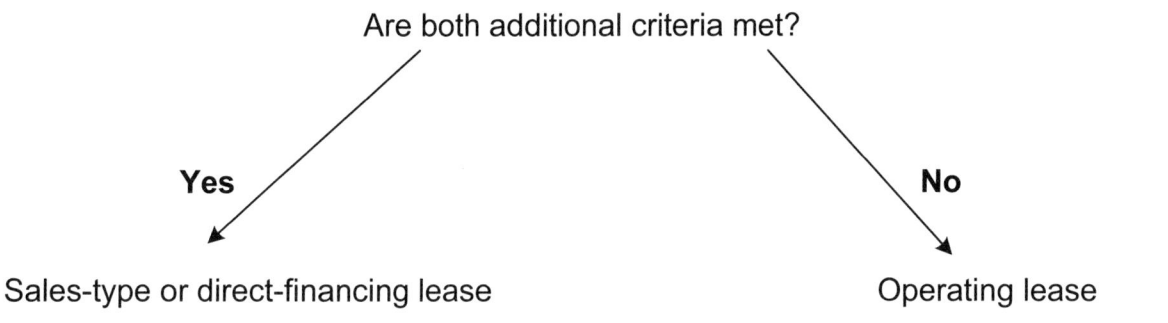

Are both additional criteria met?

Yes

Sales-type or direct-financing lease

No

Operating lease

Sales-Type & Direct-Financing Leases

Inception of lease

Journal entry to record lease:

Receivable	xxx	
Accumulated depreciation (if any)	xxx	
Asset		xxx
Gain (if any)		xxx

<u>Receivable</u> = fair value of property & present value of lease payments (rate implicit in lease)

<u>Asset & accum dep</u> – To remove carrying value of asset from lessor's books

<u>Gain</u>

- If amount needed to balance the entry, it is a gain or loss and this is a sales-type lease
- If the entry balances without a gain or loss, this is a direct financing lease

Collections

At inception of lease:

    Cash   xxx

        Receivable   xxx

Subsequent collections:

    Cash   xxx

        Interest income (formula)   xxx

        Receivable   xxx

Interest amount:

    Balance of receivable

    × Interest rate (implicit in lease)

    × Time since last payment (usually 1 year)

    = Interest amount

Balance Sheet Presentation

Receivable

- Current asset – Principal collections due within one year
- Noncurrent asset – Remainder

Operating Leases

Lessor Accounting

Rent revenue

Various expenses (depreciation on asset, taxes, insurance, & maintenance)

Lessee Accounting

Rent expense

Miscellaneous expenses (taxes, insurance, & maintenance)

Rent revenue or expense

- Recognized uniformly over lease
- Total of rents over term of lease ÷ Number of periods = Rent per period

Sale-Leaseback Transactions

Minor Leaseback

Leaseback ≤ 10% of fair value of property sold

- Sale and leaseback recognized as separate transactions
- Gain or loss on sale

Other Leasebacks

Seller-lessee retains significant portion of property

- Some or all of gain deferred
- Deferred amount limited to present value of leaseback payments
- Deferred amount spread over lease
- Remainder recognized in period of sale

Bonds

Issuance – Interest date

Cash (present value approach)	xxx		
Discount or premium (plug)	xxx	or	xxx
Bonds payable (face amount)			xxx

Issuance – Between interest dates

Cash (sales price approach + interest amount)	xxx		
Discount or premium (plug)	xxx	or	xxx
Interest payable (interest amount)			xxx
Bonds payable (face)			xxx

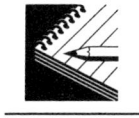

Proceeds

Present value approach

      Present value of principal (lump sum) at yield rate

  +   Present value of interest (ordinary annuity) at yield rate

Sales price approach

- Sales price given as percentage of face amount

- Multiplied by face to give proceeds amount

Interest

Bond issued between interest dates

Calculated amount

      Face amount of bonds

  ×   Stated rate

  ×   Portion of year since previous interest date

  =   Interest amount

Bond Interest

Effective interest method - GAAP

Interest payable
   Face amount
× Stated rate
× Portion of year since
   previous interest date
= Interest payable

Interest expense
   Carrying value
× Yield rate
× Portion of year since
   previous interest date
= Interest expense

Difference
Amortization of discount or premium

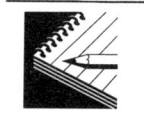

Straight-line method – Not GAAP

Interest payable
   Face amount
× Stated rate
× Portion of year since
   previous interest date
= Interest payable

Amortization
   Premium or discount
÷ Months in bond term
= Amortization per month
   interest date
× Months since last interest date
= Amortization

Interest expense = interest payable ± amortization

-   + Amortization of discount
-   − Amortization of premium

Recording Interest Expense:

Interest expense	xxx		
Bond premium or discount (amortization)	xxx	or	xxx
Cash or interest payable			xxx

Bond Issue Costs

Recorded as asset

- Deferred charge
- Amortized (straight-line) over term of bond
- Not considered part of carrying value

Bond Retirement

Bond payable (face amount)	xxx		
Bond premium or discount (balance)	xxx	or	xxx
Gain or loss (plug)	xxx	or	xxx
Bond issue costs (balance)			xxx
Cash (amount paid)			xxx

Gain or loss is extraordinary **if** retirement is determined to be both unusual and infrequent

Convertible Bonds

Recorded as bonds that are not convertible

Upon conversion:

Book Value Method		
Bonds payable (face)	xx	
Prem or disc (bal)	xx or xx	
Com stk (par)		xx
APIC (diff)		xx

Market Value Method		
Bonds payable (face)	xx	
Prem or disc (bal)	xx or xx	
Com stk (par)		xx
APIC (computed)		xx
Gain or loss (diff)	xx or xx	

Book value method
- Issuance price of stock = Carrying value of bonds
- No gain or loss

Market value method
- Issue price of stock = Fair market value
- Gain or loss recognized

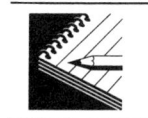

Detachable Warrants

Allocate proceeds using relative fair value method

$\qquad$ Fair value of bonds (without warrants)

$+$ $\quad$ Fair value of warrants (without bonds)

$=$ $\quad$ Total fair value

Bonds = Proceeds × Value of bonds/total value

Warrants = Proceeds × Value of warrants/total value

Record issuance:

Cash (total proceeds)	xx	
Discount or premium (plug**)	xx or xx	
$\quad$ APIC (amount allocated to warrants)		xx
$\quad$ Bonds payable (face amount)	xx	

** Bonds payable − Discount or plus premium = Amount allocated to bonds

Disclosures

A bond issuer should disclose:

- The face amount of bonds
- The nature and terms of the bonds including a discussion of credit and market risk, cash requirements, and related accounting policies
- The fair value of the bonds at the balance sheet date, indicated as a reasonable estimate of fair value

Troubled Debt Restructuring

Transfer property to creditor

Liability (amount forgiven)	xxx	
Gain or loss on disposal	xxx or	xxx
Asset (carrying value)		xxx
Extraordinary gain on restructure		xxx

Gain (or loss) on disposal = Fair value of asset – Carrying value of asset

Gain on restructure = Carrying value of debt – Fair value of asset

Issuance of equity

Liability (amount forgiven)	xxx	
Common stock (par value)		xxx
APIC (based on fair value)		xxx
Gain on restructure		xxx

APIC = Fair value of stock issued – Par value of stock issued

Gain on restructure = Fair value of stock – Carrying value of debt

Modification of Terms

Total payments under new terms:

- If ≥ carrying value of debt – no adjustment made
- If < carrying value of debt – difference is gain

Treatment of restructuring gain

Reported in ordinary income unless it is determined that the restructuring is both unusual and infrequent.

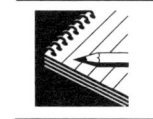

Bankruptcy

Order of distribution:

1) Fully secured creditors
   - Receive payment in full
   - Excess of fair value of asset over debt added to remaining available money
2) Partially secured creditors
   - Receive payment equal to fair value of collateral
   - Difference considered unsecured debt
3) Unsecured creditors
   - All receive partial payment
   - Remaining available money ÷ Total of unsecured claims = Ratio
   - Ratio multiplied by each claim to determine payment

Pension Plans

Pension Expense

      Service cost (debit)

+   Interest (debit

−   Actual return on plan assets (CPA exam assumes positive returns, so credit)

+   Unexpected losses (credit) /unexpected gains (debit)

±   Amortization of prior service cost (debit)

±   Corridor amortization of gains (credit) or losses (debit) in Accumulated Other Comprehensive Income (AOCI)

=   Pension expense

Pension Plans (continued)

Service cost – Increase in plan's projected benefit obligation (PBO) resulting from services performed by employees

Interest – Beginning PBO × discount (interest) rate

Actual return on plan assets – Increase in plan assets after eliminating contributions and adding back distributions

Gains or losses – 2 components

- Difference between actual return and expected return
- Amortization of AOCI for Gains/Losses in amount when beginning balance > greater of 10% of beginning PBO or 10% of market related value of beginning plan assets

Pension Plans (continued)

No longer report Prepaid or Accrued Pension Liability

Instead, report on Balance Sheet difference between fair value of plan assets and the PBO as a noncurrent asset if overfunded and a noncurrent liability if underfunded.

Minimum liability test no longer reported

Disclosures

- Description of funding policies and types of assets held: equity, debt, real estate and other
- Six components of Pension expense for the period
- Expected benefits to be paid each of the next five years and in aggregate for the following five years
- Expected cash contribution for the following year

Postretirement Benefits

Types of Benefits

Company pays for:
- Health care
- Tuition assistance
- Legal services
- Life insurance
- Day care
- Housing subsidies

Individuals covered:
- Retired employees
- Beneficiaries
- Covered dependents

Postretirement Benefit Expense

     Service cost (debit)

+   Interest (debit)

−   Actual return on plan assets (CPA exam assumes positive returns, so credit)

+   Unexpected losses (credit) /unexpected gains (debit)

±   Amortization of prior service cost (debit)

±   Corridor amortization of gains (credit) or losses (debit) in Accumulated Other Comprehensive Income (AOCI)

=   Postretirement benefit expense

Accounting for Income Taxes (FAS 109)

Income Tax Expense

Taxable income = Pretax accounting income

- No temporary differences
- Income tax expense = Current income tax expense
- No deferred tax effect

Taxable income ≠ Pretax accounting income

- Temporary differences
- Income tax expense = Current income tax expense ± Deferred income taxes

Current Income Tax

Current income tax expense = Taxable income × Current tax rate

Current tax liability = Current income tax expense − Estimated payments

Taxable income:

      Pretax accounting income (financial statement income)

±   Permanent differences

±   Changes in cumulative amounts of temporary differences

=   Taxable income

Permanent & Temporary Differences

Permanent differences

- Nontaxable income (interest income on municipal bonds) & nondeductible expenses (premiums on officers' life insurance)
- No income tax effect

Temporary differences

- Carrying values of assets or liabilities ≠ tax bases
- May be taxable temporary differences (TTD) or deductible temporary differences (DTD)

Assets

Financial statement basis > tax basis = TTD
Financial statement basis < tax basis = DTD

Liabilities

Financial statement basis > tax basis = DTD
Financial statement basis < tax basis = TTD

Deferred Tax Assets & Liabilities

TTD × Enacted future tax rate = Deferred tax liability

DTD × Enacted future tax rate = Deferred tax asset

Selecting appropriate rate:

1) Determine future period when temporary difference will have tax effect (period of reversal)
2) Determine enacted tax rate for that period

Deferred Tax Asset Valuation Allowance

May apply to any deferred tax asset

- Is it more likely than not that some or all of deferred tax asset will not be realized
- Consider tax planning strategies

Valuation allowance = portion of deferred tax asset that will not be realized

Deferred Income Tax Expense or Benefit

1) Calculate balances of deferred tax liabilities and assets and valuation allowances
2) Combine into single net amount
3) Compare to combined amount at beginning of period
   - Increase in net liability amount = deferred income tax expense
   - Decrease in net asset amount = deferred income tax expense
   - Increase in net asset amount = deferred income tax benefit
   - Decrease in net liability amount = deferred income tax benefit

Balance Sheet Presentation

Identify current and noncurrent deferred tax assets, liabilities, and valuation allowances

Current – TTD or DTD relates to asset or liability classified as current

Noncurrent – TTD or DTD relates to asset or liability classified as noncurrent

TTD or DTD does not relate to specific asset or liability (such as result of net operating loss carryforward) – classify as current or noncurrent depending on period of tax effect

1) Combine current deferred tax assets, liabilities, and valuation allowances into single amount
2) Report as current deferred tax asset or liability
3) Combine noncurrent deferred tax assets, liabilities, and valuation allowances into single amount
4) Report as noncurrent deferred tax asset or liability

FIN 48: Accounting for Uncertainty in Income Taxes

- Applies to all tax positions related to income taxes subject to FAS 109
- Utilizes a two-step approach for evaluating tax positions.
  - Recognition (Step 1) occurs when an enterprise concludes that a tax position, based solely on its technical merits, is more likely than not to be sustained upon examination.
  - Measurement (Step 2) is only addressed if Step 1 has been maintained. Under Step 2, the tax benefit is measured as the largest amount of benefit, determined on a cumulative probability basis, that is more likely than not to be realized (i.e., a likelihood of occurrence greater than 50%)
  - Those tax positions failing to qualify for initial recognition under Step 1 are recognized in the first subsequent interim period that they meet the more-likely-than-not standard, and are resolved through negotiation or litigation or on expiration of the statute of limitations.

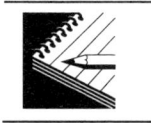

FIN 48: Accounting for Uncertainty in Income Taxes (continued)

- Derecognition of a tax position that was previously recognized occurs when the item fails to meet more-likely-than-not threshold.
- FIN 48 specifically prohibits the use of a deferred tax valuation allowance as a substitute for derecognition of tax positions

Stockholders' Equity

Issuance of Common Stock

Stock issued for cash, property, or services:

Journal entry:

Cash, property, or expense (fair value)	xxx	
Common stock (par or stated value)		xxx
APIC (difference)		xxx

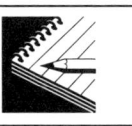

Common Stock Subscribed

Subscription – Journal entry:

Cash (down payment)	xxx	
Subscriptions receivable (balance)	xxx	
Common stock subscribed (par or stated value)		xxx
APIC (difference)		xxx

Collection and issuance of shares – Journal entries:

Cash (balance)	xxx	
Subscriptions receivable		xxx
Common stock subscribed (par or stated value)	xxx	
Common stock (par or stated value)		xxx

Treasury Stock

Acquisition of shares:

<u>Cost Method</u>

TS (cost)	xx	
Cash		xx

<u>Par Value Method</u>

TS (par value)	xx
APIC (original amount)	xx
RE (difference)	xx

or

APIC from TS (difference)	xx
Cash (cost)	xx

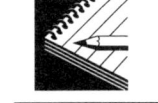

Acquisition of shares (continued)

Sale – more than cost:

Cost Method			*Par Value Method*		
Cash (proceeds)	xx		Cash (proceeds)	xx	
TS (cost)		xx	TS (par)		xx
APIC from TS		xx	APIC (difference)		xx

Sale – less than cost:

Cost Method		*Par Value Method*
Cash (proceeds)	xx	Same entry as above
APIC from TS (difference		
up to balance)	xx	
RE (remainder of difference)	xx	
TS (cost)	xx	

Characteristics of Preferred Stock

Preference over common stock

- Receive dividends prior to common stockholders

- Paid before common on liquidation

Cumulative preferred stock

- Unpaid dividends accumulated as dividends in arrears

- Paid in subsequent periods prior to payment of current dividends to common or pre-ferred

- Not considered liability until declared

Participating preferred stock

- Receive current dividends prior to common stockholders

- Receive additional dividends, in proportion to common stockholders, in periods of high dividends

Equity Instruments with Characteristics of Liabilities

Financial instruments shares should be classified as liabilities on the balance sheet, even when they appear to be in the form of equity, when any of these characteristics apply:

- Preferred shares have a mandatory redemption date payable in cash
- An obligation exists to repurchase shares through the transfer of assets to the shareholder.
- Shares are convertible to other shares when the exchange rate is based on a fixed monetary value of issuer shares or is tied to variations in the fixed value of something other than the issuer's shares.

Note that convertible shares whose conversion rate is not adjusted for changes in values do not fall into this category (e.g. preferred stock convertible at a fixed 10 for 1 ratio to the common stock would not be a liability)

Dividends

Cash Dividends

Recorded when declared

1) Dividends in arrears to preferred stockholders if cumulative
2) Normal current dividend to preferred stockholders
3) Comparable current dividend to common stockholders
4) Remainder
   - Allocated between common and preferred shares if preferred stock is participating
   - Paid to common stockholders if preferred stock is nonparticipating

Property Dividends

Journal entry

Retained earnings (fmv of property)	xxx	
Gain (or loss)	xxx or xxx	
Asset (carrying value of property)		xxx

Liquidating Dividends

Journal entry

Retained earnings (balance)	xxx	
APIC (plug)	xxx	
Cash or Dividends payable		xxx

Stock Dividends

Journal entry - Normal stock dividend – usually 20% or less

Retained earnings (fmv of stock issued)	xxx	
Common stock (par or stated value)		xxx
APIC (difference)		xxx

Journal entry – Large stock dividend – usually more than 25% – referred to as stock split affected in the form of a stock dividend

Retained earnings (par or stated value)	xxx	
Common stock (par or stated value)		xxx

Preferred Stock – Special Issuances

Preferred with Detachable Warrants

Cash (proceeds)	xxx	
APIC from warrants (amount allocated)		xxx
Preferred stock (par)		xxx
APIC from preferred stock (difference)		xxx

Amount allocated to warrants using relative fair value method:

      Fair value of warrants

+   Fair value of stock

=   Total fair value

Allocation:

- Fair value of warrants ÷ Total fair value × Proceeds = Amount allocated to warrants
- Fair value of stock ÷ Total fair value × Proceeds = Amount allocated to stock

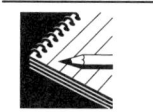

Convertible Preferred Stock

Journal entry – Issuance

Cash (proceeds)	xxx	
Preferred stock (par)		xxx
APIC from preferred stock (difference)		xxx

Journal entry – Conversion

Preferred stock (par)	xxx	
APIC from preferred stock (original amount)	xxx	
Common stock (par or stated value)		xxx
APIC (difference)		xxx

Retained Earnings

Appropriations

Set up to disclose to financial statement users future commitments that are not subject to accrual.

Journal entry:

Retained earnings	xxx	
Retained earnings appropriated for…		xxx

When the commitment is met, accrued, or avoided, the appropriation is reversed.

Journal entry:

Retained earnings appropriated for…	xxx	
Retained earnings		xxx

Prior Period Adjustments

Made to correct errors in financial statements of prior periods

Adjustment to beginning retained earnings

- Equal to net amount of errors from periods prior to earliest period presented
- Reduced by tax effect

Presented on statement of retained earnings

- Unadjusted beginning balance reported
- Increased or decreased for prior period adjustment
- Result is adjusted beginning balance

Statement of Retained Earnings

	Beginning retained earnings, as previously reported	xxx
±	Prior period adjustments	<u>xxx</u>
=	Beginning retained earnings, as adjusted	xxx
+	Net income for period	xxx
−	Dividends	xxx
−	Appropriations	xxx
+	Appropriations eliminated	<u>xxx</u>
=	Ending retained earnings	<u>xxx</u>

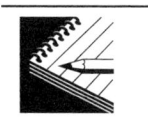

Stock Options Plans

Noncompensatory Plans

Noncompensatory when:

- All employees participate
- Participation uniform among employees
- Option period limited to reasonable time
- Discount below market price limited to reasonable amount

Compensatory Plans

Journal entry

Deferred compensation	xxx	
APIC – Options		xxx

Options must be accounted for using FMV at date of grant based on:

- Market price of options with similar characteristics
- Option pricing model
    - Binomial distribution model
    - Black-Scholes model
- Intrinsic value (stock price – exercise price) only used when FMV cannot be determined at grant date and must be replaced by FMV as soon as estimate is available

Compensation recognized over service period

Stock Appreciation Rights

Calculating liability

      Stock price

− Amount specified in stock appreciation rights

= Amount per share

× # of stock appreciation rights

= Total liability

× Portion of service period elapsed

= Liability on balance sheet date

Amount needed to increase or decrease liability is recognized as compensation expense

Quasi Reorganizations

Journal entry:

Common stock (reduction in par value)	xxx		
APIC (plug)	xxx	or	xxx
Retained earnings (eliminate deficit)			xxx
Assets (eliminate overstatements)			xxx

Book Value Per Share

Calculation:

Total stockholders' equity

$-$ Preferred stock (par value or liquidation preference)

$-$ Dividends in arrears on cumulative preferred stock

$=$ Stockholders' equity attributable to common stockholders

$\div$ Common shares outstanding at balance sheet date

$=$ Book value per common share

Disclosure of Information About Capital Structure

Rights & privileges of various debt & equity securities outstanding

- Number of shares of common and preferred stock authorized, issued, & outstanding
- Dividend & liquidation preferences
- Participation rights
- Call prices & dates
- Conversion or exercise prices or rates & pertinent dates
- Sinking fund requirements
- Unusual voting rights
- Significant terms of contracts to issue additional shares

Reporting Stockholders' Equity

6% cumulative preferred stock, $100 par value, 200,000 shares authorized, 120,000 shares issued and outstanding		$ 12,000,000
Common stock, $10 par value, 1,500,000 shares authorized, 1,150,000 shares issued and 1,090,000 shares outstanding		11,500,000
Additional paid-in capital		3,650,000
		27,150,000
Retained Earnings:		
Unappropriated	$ 6,925,000	
Retained earnings appropriated for plant expansion	1,400,000	8,325,000
Accumulated other comprehensive income:		
Accumulated unrealized gain due to increase In value of marketable securities available for sale	750,000	
Accumulated translation adjustment	(515,000)	235,000
		35,710,000
Less: Treasury stock, 60,000 shares at cost		780,000
Total Stockholders' Equity		$ 34,930,000

Earnings Per Share

Reporting Earnings Per Share

Simple capital structure

- No potentially dilutive securities outstanding
- Present basic EPS only

Complex capital structure

- Potentially dilutive securities outstanding
- Dual presentation of EPS – basic EPS & diluted EPS

Potentially dilutive securities - Securities that can be converted into common shares

- Convertible bonds and convertible preferred stock
- Options, rights, and warrants

Basic EPS

Numerator - Income Available to Common Stockholders

Income from continuing operations

- − Dividends declared on noncumulative preferred stock
- − Current dividends on cumulative preferred stock (whether or not declared)
- = Income from continuing operations available to common stockholders
- ± Discontinued operations
- ± Extraordinary items
- = Net income available to common stockholders

Denominator

Weighted-average common shares outstanding on the balance sheet date

Diluted EPS

Adjust numerator & denominator for dilutive securities
- Assume conversion into common shares
- Dilutive if EPS decreases

Convertible Preferred Stock

Dilutive if basic EPS is greater than preferred dividend per share of common stock obtainable:
- Add preferred dividends back to numerator
- Add common shares that preferred would be converted into to denominator

Convertible Bonds

Dilutive if basic EPS is greater than interest, net of tax, per share of common stock obtainable:
- Add interest, net of tax, to numerator
- Add common shares that bonds would be converted into to denominator

Options, Rights, & Warrants

Dilutive when market price exceeds exercise price (proceeds from exercise)

The **treasury stock method** is applied

Number of options ————————————→ Number of options
 × Exercise price
 = Proceeds from exercise
 ÷ Average market price of stock during period
 = Shares reacquired with proceeds ————————→ − Shares reacquired
 = Increase in denominator

Calculation done on quarter-by-quarter basis

Presentation of EPS Information

Income Statement

Simple capital structure – Basic EPS only
- Income from continuing operations
- Net income

Complex capital structure – Basic & Diluted EPS
- Income from continuing operations
- Net income

Additional Disclosures (income statement or notes)

- Discontinued operations
- Extraordinary items

Methods of Reporting Investments

Method	Conditions
Consolidation	Majority owned (> 50%)
Equity	Less than majority owned Ability to exercise significant influence Ownership generally ≥ 20%
Cost	Less than majority owned Unable to exercise significant influence Ownership generally < 20% Not an investment in marketable securities
Special Rules (FASB #115)	Less than majority owned Unable to exercise significant influence Ownership generally < 20% Investment in marketable securities

Equity Method

Carrying Value of Investment

Cost
+ Earnings
− Dividends
= Carrying value of investment

Earnings

Income reported by investee
× % of ownership
= Unadjusted amount
  • Adjustments
= Investor's share of investee's earnings

Equity Method

Adjustments to Earnings

1) Compare initial investment to FMV of underlying net assets
2) Portion of excess may be due to inventory

    Deduct from income in the first year (unless inventory not sold during year)
3) Portion of excess may be due to depreciable asset

    Divide by useful life and deduct from income each year
4) Portion of excess may be due to land

    No adjustment (unless land sold during year)
5) Remainder of excess attributed to goodwill

    Test each year for impairment and deduct from income if it has occurred

Equity Method

Application of Equity Method

Information given:

Investment	25%
Cost	$400,000
Book value of investee's underlying net assets	$900,000
Undervalued assets:	
Inventory	100,000
Building (20 yrs)	400,000
Land	200,000
Investee's unadjusted income	$225,000
Dividends	$40,000

Application of Equity Method (continued)

Information Applied

Value of investment $- $400,000 \div 25\%$ $1,6000,000

Book value of underlying net assets   900,000

    Difference $\underline{\ \ 700,000}$

Reconciliation of difference			*Earnings adjustment*
Inventory	$100,000		$100,000
Building	400,000	÷ 20	20,000
Land	200,000		
Total	$700,000		$120,000

Earnings

			Carrying value	
Income reported by investee	$225,000		Cost	$400,000
• Adjustments	(120,000)		+ Earnings	26,250
= Adjusted amount	105,000		− Dividends	
× % of ownership	25%		($40,000 × 25%)	10,000
= Investor's share	$26,250		= Carrying value	$416,250

Changes to and from the Equity Method

Equity Method to Cost Method

- No longer able to exercise significant influence
- Usually associated with sale of portion of investment
- Apply equity method to date of change
- Apply cost method from date of change

Cost Method to Equity Method

- Now able to exercise significant influence
- Usually associated with additional purchase
- Apply equity method retroactively
- Affects retained earnings and investment for prior periods

Marketable Securities

	Trading Securities	Available for Sale	Held to Maturity
Types of securities in classification	Debt or equity	Debt or equity	Debt only
Balance sheet classification	Current	Current or noncurrent	Noncurrent until maturity
Carrying amount on balance sheet	Fair market value	Fair market value	Cost, net of amortization
Unrealized gains and losses	Income statement	Equity section of balance sheet *	Not applicable
Realized gains and losses	Income statement	Income statement	Should not occur

* Excluded from net income – included in comprehensive income

Life Insurance

Payment of premium:

Cash surrender value of life insurance (increase in value)	xxx	
Insurance expense (plug)	xxx	
Cash (premium amount)		xxx

Death of insured:

Cash (face of policy)	xxx	
Cash surrender value of life insurance (balance)		xxx
Gain (difference)		xxx

Statement of Cash Flows

Purpose of Statement

Summarizes sources and uses of cash and **cash equivalents**

Classifies cash flows into operating, investing, and financing activities

Cash Equivalents

Easily converted into cash (liquid)

Original maturity ≤ 3 months

Format of Statement

Cash provided or (used) by **operating** activities

±   Cash provided or (used) by **investing** activities

±   Cash provided or (used) by **financing** activities

=   Net increase or (decrease) in cash & cash equivalents

+   Beginning balance

=   Ending balance

Operating Activities

Direct Method – Top to bottom

    Collections from customers
+   Interest & dividends received
+   Proceeds from sale of trading securities
+   Other operating cash inflows
−   Payments for merchandise
−   Payments for expense
−   Payments for interest
−   Payments for income taxes
−   Payments to acquire trading securities
−   Other operating cash outflows

=   **Cash flows from operating activities**

Direct Method – Top to bottom

Net income
Noncash revenues −
Noncash expenses +
Gains on sales of investments −
Losses on sales of investments +
Gains on sales of plant assets −
Losses on sales of plant assets +
Increases in current assets −
Decreases in current assets +
Decreases in current liabilities −
Increases in current liabilities +

Cash flows from operating activities =

Must be equal

Components of Direct Method

Collections from customers (plug)   xxx
Increase in accounts receivable (given)   xxx
   Decrease in accounts receivable (given)   xxx
   Sales (given)   xxx

Increase in inventory (given)   xxx
Decrease in accounts payable (given)   xxx
Cost of sales (given)   xxx
   Decrease in inventory (given)   xxx
   Increase in accounts payable (given)   xxx
   Payments for merchandise (plug)   xxx

Adjustments Under Indirect Method

- Credit changes are addbacks/debit changes are subtractions, for example
  - Increase in accumulated depreciation added back
  - Increase in accounts payable added back
  - Increase in accounts receivable subtracted
  - Decrease in accounts payable subtracted

Investing Activities

Principal collections on loans receivable

+ Proceeds from sale of investments (except trading securities)

+ Proceeds from sale of plant assets

− Loans made

− Payments to acquire investments (except trading securities)

− Payments to acquire plant assets

= **Cash flows from investing activities**

Financing Activities

Proceeds from borrowings

\+   Proceeds from issuing stock

−   Debt principal payments

−   Payments to reacquire stock

−   Payments for dividends

=   **Cash flows from financing activities**

Other Disclosures

With direct method:

    Reconciliation of net income to cash flows from operating activities (indirect method)

With indirect method:

    Payments for interest

    Payments for income taxes

With all cash flow statements:

    Schedule of noncash investing and financing activities

Business Combinations

Consolidation is required whenever the Acquirer has control over another entity.

- Acquirer is the entity that obtains control of one or more businesses in the business combination
- Ownership of majority of voting stock generally indicates control
- Consolidation is required even if control situation is temporary
- Consolidation is not appropriate when a majority shareholder doesn't have effective control:
  - Company is in bankruptcy or reorganization
  - Foreign exchange controls limit power to keep control of subsidiary assets
- All consolidations are accounted for as purchases
  - The acquirer shall recognize, goodwill, the identifiable assets acquired, the liabilities assumed, any noncontrolling interest in the acquiree, and any residual goodwill
  - Recognize separately
    - Acquisition-related costs

Business Combinations (continued)

- Assets acquired and liabilities assumed arising from *contractual contingencies*
- Bargain purchase (fair value of assets acquired > amount paid) recognized as gain
- Fair values of research and development assets
- Changes in the value of acquirer deferred tax benefits

Accounting for a Purchase

Combination – Records combined

Assets (at fair market values)	xxx	
Separately identifiable assets	xx	
Goodwill (plug)	x	
Liabilities (at fair market values)		xxx
Stockholders' equity (2 steps) *		xxx
OR		
Cash (amount paid)		xxx

* Credit common stock for par value of shares issued and credit APIC for difference between fair value and par value of shares issued

Combination – Records not combined

Investment (fair value of net assets)	xxx	
Stockholders' equity (same 2 steps)		xxx
OR		
Cash (amount paid)		xxx

Earnings

Consolidated net income:

> Parent's net income

+ Subsidiary's net income from date of acquisition

± Effects of intercompany transactions

− Depreciation on difference between fair value and carrying value of sub's assets

− Impairment losses on goodwill (if applicable)

= Consolidated net income

Retained Earnings - Year of Combination

    Beginning retained earnings – Parent's beginning balance

+   Consolidated net income

−   Parent's dividends for entire period

=   Ending retained earnings

Consolidations

Eliminate the Investment

Example 1 – Date of combination – no goodwill or minority interest

Inventory (excess of fair value over carrying value)	**xxx**	
Land (excess of fair value over carrying value)	**xxx**	
Depreciable assets (excess of fair value over Carrying value)	**xxx**	
Common stock (sub's balance)	xxx	
APIC (sub's balance)	xxx	
Retained earnings (sub's balance)	xxx	
Investment		xxx

Example 2 – Date of combination – no goodwill with minority interest

Inventory (excess of fair value over carrying value)	xxx	
Land (excess of fair value over carrying value)	xxx	
Depreciable assets (excess of fair value over carrying value)	xxx	
Common stock (sub's balance)	xxx	
APIC (sub's balance)	xxx	
Retained earnings (sub's balance)	xxx	
Minority interest (sub's total stockholders' equity × minority interest percentage)		**xxx**
Investment		xxx

Example 3 – Date of combination – goodwill and minority interest

Inventory (excess of fair value over carrying value)	xxx
Land (excess of fair value over carrying value)	xxx
Depreciable assets (excess of fair value over carrying value)	xxx
Goodwill (plug)	**xxx**
Common stock (sub's balance)	xxx
APIC (sub's balance)	xxx
Retained earnings (sub's balance)	xxx
Minority interest (sub's total stockholders' equity × minority interest percentage)	xxx
Investment	xxx

Calculating goodwill – 4 steps

1) Determine amount paid for acquisition

2) Compare to book value of sub's underlying net assets

3) Subtract difference between fair values and book values of sub's assets

4) Remainder is goodwill

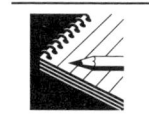

Eliminate the Investment (continued)

Additional entries – after date of acquisition

- Debit cost of sales instead of inventory for fair market value adjustment
- Recognize depreciation on excess of fair value over carrying value of depreciable assets
- Recognize impairment of goodwill (if FMV of goodwill is less than carrying amount)

Eliminating Entries

Intercompany Sales of Inventory

Eliminate gross amount of intercompany sales

Sales	xxx	
Cost of sales		xxx

Eliminate intercompany profit included in ending inventory

Cost of sales	xxx	
Inventory		xxx

Eliminate unpaid portion of intercompany sales

Accounts payable	xxx	
Accounts receivable		xxx

Intercompany Sales of Property, Plant, & Equipment

Eliminate intercompany gain or loss

    Gain on sale (amount recognized)   xxx

        Depreciable asset   xxx

Adjust depreciation

    Accumulated depreciation (amount of gain
    divided by remaining useful life)   xxx

        Depreciation expense   xxx

Intercompany Bond Holdings

Eliminate intercompany investment in bonds

    Bonds payable (face amount of bonds acquired)   xxx

    Bond premium or discount (amount related to
    Intercompany bonds)   xxx or xxx

        Gain or loss on retirement (plug)   xxx or xxx

        Investment in bonds (carrying value)   xxx

Investments in Derivative Securities

Derivatives – Derive their value from other assets. Examples:

- Stock option – value based on underlying stock price
- Commodity futures contract – value based on underlying commodity price

Initially recorded at cost (or allocated amount) – Reported on balance sheet at fair value

- Trading security – unrealized gains and losses on income statement
- Available for sale security – unrealized gains and losses reported as other comprehensive income in stockholders' equity

Characteristics of Derivatives

Settlement in cash or assets easily convertible to cash (such as marketable securities)

Underlying index on which value of derivative is based (usually the price of some asset)

No net investment at time of creation:

- Futures-based derivative involves no payments at all when derivative created
    - Such a derivative must be settled on settlement date in all cases
- Options-based derivative involves small premium payment when derivative created
    - Option holder has right not to settle derivative if results would be unfavorable
    - Payment of premium when derivative created is price of this option.

Use of Derivatives

Speculative – Attempt to profit from favorable change in underlying index

- Gain or loss on change in fair value reported in ordinary income

Fair Value Hedge – Attempt to offset risk of existing asset, liability, or commitment

- Hedge must move in opposite direction to offsetting item
- Movement must be between 80% and 125% of offsetting item to be effective hedge
- Gain or loss on change in derivative reported in ordinary income
  - Should approximately offset loss or gain on item being hedged

Cash Flow Hedge – Attempt to offset risk associated with future expected transactions

- Gain or loss excluded from ordinary income until offsetting future event affects income
  - Reported as part of other comprehensive income until that time

Financial Instruments

Risk of loss:

Market risk – Losses due to fluctuations in market place

Credit risk – Losses due to nonperformance of other party

Concentration of credit risk – Several instruments have common characteristics resulting in similar risks

Required Disclosures

- Off-balance-sheet credit risk – credit risk that is not already reflected as an accrued contingency
- Concentration of credit risk

Fair Value Option and Measurements

The fair value option

- May be applied instrument by instrument, with a few exceptions, such as investments otherwise accounted for by the equity method

- Is irrevocable

- Is applied only to entire instruments and not to portions of instruments

Available for

- Recognized financial assets and financial liabilities with the following major exceptions:

    - An investment in a subsidiary that the entity is required to consolidate

    - Pension and other postretirement benefit plans including employee stock plans

    - Lease assets and liabilities

    - Deposit liabilities, of banks, savings and loan associations, credit unions, etc.

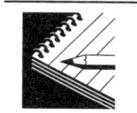

The fair value option (continued)

- Firm commitments that would otherwise not be recognized at inception and that involve only financial instruments

- Nonfinancial insurance contracts and warranties that the insurer can settle by paying a third party to provide those goods or services

- Host financial instruments resulting from separation of an embedded nonfinancial derivative instrument from a nonfinancial hybrid instrument

Recognize unrealized gains and losses in earnings for businesses and in statement of activities for nonprofit organizations.

Fair Value defined

- Exchange price

  - Orderly transaction between market participants to sell the asset or transfer the liability the principal or most advantageous market for the asset or liability

  - Value is a market-based measurement, not an entity-specific measurement

  - Includes assumptions about

Fair Value defined (continued)

- Risk inherent in a particular valuation technique or inputs to the valuation technique

- Effect of a restriction on the sale or use of an asset

- Nonperformance risk

Expanded disclosures on the inputs used to measure fair value

Level 1

- Quoted prices in active markets for identical assets or liabilities

Level 2

- Inputs such as quoted prices on similar assets or liabilities or observable for the asset or liability such as interest rates and yield curves

Level 3

- Unobservable inputs for the asset or liability that reflect the reporting entity's own assumptions about the assumptions that market participants would use in pricing the asset or liability (including assumptions about risk).

Segment Reporting

Definition of Segments

Segments identified using management approach:

- Component earns revenue and incurs expenses
- Separate information is available
- Component is evaluated regularly by top management

Reportable Segments - 3 Tests

Revenue test – Segment revenues $\geq$ 10% of total revenues

Asset test – Segment identifiable assets $\geq$ 10% of total assets

Profit or loss test

- Combine profits for all profitable segments
- Combine losses for all losing segments
- Select larger amount
- Segments profit or loss $\geq$ 10% of larger amount

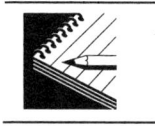

Disclosures for Reportable Segments

Segment profit or loss
- Segment revenues include intersegment sales
- Deduct traceable operating expenses and allocated indirect operating expenses
- Do not deduct general corporate expenses

Segment revenues

Segment assets

Interest revenue & expense

Depreciation, depletion, & amortization

Other items

Partnership

Admitting a Partner

Calculating the Contribution – No Goodwill or Bonus

       Partnership equity (before new partner's contribution)

$\div$ 100% – new partner's percentage

$=$ Total capital after contribution

$\times$ New partner's percentage

$=$ Amount to be contributed

Journal entry:

Cash	xxx	
New partner's equity		xxx

Excess Contribution by New Partner – Bonus Method

        Partnership equity (before new partner's contribution)

+	New partner's contribution	New partner's contribution
=	Total capital after contribution	
×	New partner's percentage	
=	New partner's capital	− New partner's capital
		= Bonus to existing partners

Journal entry:

Cash (new partner's contribution)	xxx	
Capital, new partner (amount calculated)		xxx
Capital, existing partners (bonus amount)		xxx

Bonus is allocated to existing partners using their P & L percentages

Excess Contribution by New Partner – Goodwill Method

      New partner's contribution

÷ New partner's percentage

= Total capital after contribution

− Total capital of partnership (existing capital + contribution)

= Goodwill to existing partners

Journal entry:

Cash (new partner's contribution)	xxx	
Capital, new partner (new partner's contribution)		xxx
Goodwill (amount calculated)	xxx	
Capital, existing partners		xxx

Goodwill is allocated to existing partners using their P & L percentages

Contribution Below New Partner's Capital – Bonus Method

    Partnership equity (before new partner's contribution)
+ New partner's contribution
= Total capital after contribution
× New partner's percentage
= New partner's capital
− New partner's contribution
= Bonus to new partner

Journal entry:

Cash (new partner's contribution)	xxx
Capital, existing partners (bonus amount)	xxx
Capital, new partner (amount calculated)	xxx

Bonus is allocated to existing partners using their P & L percentages

Contribution Below New Partner's Capital – Goodwill Method

      Partnership equity (before new partner's contribution)

÷   100% - new partner's percentage

=   Total capital after contribution

×   New partner's percentage

=   New partner's capital

−   New partner's contribution

=   Goodwill

Journal entry:

Cash (new partner's contribution)	xxx	
Goodwill (amount calculated)	xxx	
Capital, new partner (total)		xxx

Retiring a Partner

Payment Exceeds Partner's Balance – Bonus Method

Capital, retiring partner (existing balance)	xxx	
Capital, remaining partners (difference – bonus)	xxx	
Cash (amount paid)		xxx

Bonus is allocated to existing partners using their P & L percentages

Payment Exceeds Partner's Balance – Goodwill Method

      Amount paid to retiring partner

÷   Retiring partner's percentage

=   Value of partnership on date of retirement

−   Partnership equity before retirement

=   Goodwill

Journal entries:

Goodwill (amount calculated)	xxx	
Capital, all partners		xxx

Goodwill is allocated according to the partners' P & L percentages

Capital, retiring partner	xxx	
Cash (amount paid to retiring partner)		xxx

Partnership Liquidation – 5 steps

1) Combine each partner's capital account with loans to or from that partner
2) Allocate gain or loss on assets sold to partners
3) Assume remaining assets are total loss – allocate to partners
4) Eliminate any partner's negative balance by allocating to remaining partners using their P & L percentages
5) Resulting balances will be amounts to be distributed to remaining partners

Foreign Currency

Foreign Currency Transactions

Receivable or payable

- Record at **spot rate**
- Adjust to new spot rate on each financial statement date

Journal entry:

Receivable or payable	xxx	
Foreign currency transaction gain		xxx
OR		
Foreign currency transaction loss	xxx	
Receivable or payable		xxx

Gain or loss = Change in spot rate × Receivable or payable (in foreign currency)

Forward Exchange Contracts

All gains and losses measured using forward rate – rate expected to be in effect when settled

Hedge – Protection against change in exchange rate related to **existing** receivable or payable

- Change in forward rate results in gain or loss on hedge
- This will approximately offset loss or gain on change in spot rate on receivable or payable

Special hedge contracts:

- Hedge of foreign currency investment – gains or losses reported in equity – excluded from net income but included in comprehensive income
- Hedge of foreign commitment – gain or loss deferred and offset against transaction

Speculative contracts – Entered into in anticipation of change in rate

- Change in forward rate results in gain or loss

Foreign Currency Financial Statements

Conversion to U.S. $:

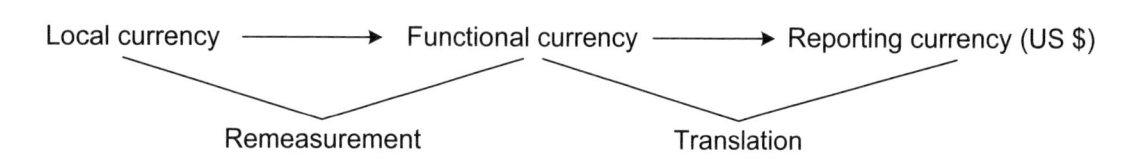

Local currency ⟶ Functional currency ⟶ Reporting currency (US $)

Remeasurement   Translation

Functional Currency – Currency of primary economic environment in which entity operates.

1) Functional currency = local currency
   - Translate from local currency to U.S. $
2) Functional currency = U.S. $
   - Remeasure from local currency to U.S. $
3) Functional currency neither local currency nor U.S. $
   - Remeasure from local currency to functional currency
   - Translate from functional currency to U.S. $

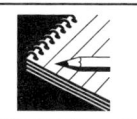

Remeasurement and Translation

Remeasurement

Historical rate:
- Nonmonetary assets and liabilities
- Contributed capital accounts
- Revenue and expense accounts

Current rate:
- All other items

Difference:
- Remeasurement gain or loss
- Reported on income statement

Translation

Rate at balance sheet date:
- Assets and liabilities

Rate in effect on transaction date
 (or weighted-average rate for period):

- Revenues and expenses
- Gains and losses

Difference:
- Translation gain or loss
- Component of stockholders' equity
- Excluded from net income
- Included in comprehensive income

Interim Financial Statements

General Rules

1) Revenues & expenses recognized in interim period earned or incurred
2) Same principles as applied to annual financial statements

Special Rules

Inventory Losses

Expected to recover within annual period

- Not recognized in interim period
- Offset against recovery in subsequent interim period
- Recognized when clear that recovery will not occur

Not expected to recover within annual period

- Recognized in interim period
- Recovery in subsequent interim period recognized

Income Taxes

Estimate of rate that applies to annual period

Other Items

Property taxes – allocated among interim periods

Repairs & maintenance

- Generally recognized in interim period when incurred (including major repairs)
- Allocated to current & subsequent interim periods when future benefit results

Disposal of a segment – recognized in interim period in which it occurs

Extraordinary item – recognized in interim period in which it occurs

Personal Financial Statements

Basic Statements

Statement of Financial Condition

Statement of Changes in Net Worth

Principles Applied

Assets & liabilities – Reported at fair market values

Business interests – Reported as single amount

Real estate
- When operated as business – reported net of mortgage
- When not operated as business – asset and mortgage reported separately

Retirement plans
- Contributions & earnings on contributions by employee included
- Contributions & earnings on contributions by employer included to extent vested

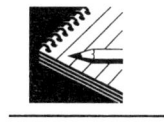

Principles Applied (continued)

Life insurance – Cash surrender value minus borrowings against policy

Income taxes – 2 components
- Income taxes on individual's income for year to date
- Tax effect on difference between tax basis and fair values of assets and liabilities

Other liabilities

- Current payoff amount, if available
- Otherwise, present value of future payments

Governmental Accounting

Objective of governmental accounting & reporting – **accountability**

- Provide useful information
- Benefit wide range of users

Governmental financial information should:

- Demonstrate operations within legal restraints imposed by citizens
- Communicate compliance with laws & regulations related to raising & spending money
- Demonstrate **interperiod equity** – current period expenditures financed with current revenues

To demonstrate full accountability for all activities, information must include:

- Cost of services
- Sufficiency of revenues for services provided
- Financial position

Funds

Government comprised of funds – self-balancing sets of accounts – 3 categories

- Governmental
- Proprietary
- Fiduciary

Methods of Accounting

Funds of a governmental unit use two methods of accounting

- Most funds use **modified accrual accounting**
- Some funds use accrual accounting

Modified Accrual Accounting

Differs from accrual accounting:

- Focus of financial reporting is financial position & flow of resources
- Revenues are recognized when they become available & measurable
- Expenditures are recorded when goods or services are obtained
- Expenditures classified by **object, function, or character**

Financial Statements of Governmental Units

General purpose financial statements – referred to as **Comprehensive Annual Financial Report (CAFR)** – 5 components

- Management discussions & analysis – Presented before financial statements
- Government-wide financial statements
- Fund financial statements
- Notes to financial statements
- Required supplementary information – Presented after financial statements and notes

Users should be able to distinguish between primary government & component units – component units may be **blended** when either:

- Governing body of component is essentially the same as that of the primary government
- The component provides services almost exclusively for the primary government

Most component units will be **discretely presented**

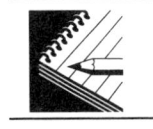

Management Discussion & Analysis (MD & A)

Introduces basic financial statements & provides analytical overview of government's financial activities

Should include:

- Condensed comparison of current year financial information to prior year
- Analysis of overall financial position and results of operations
- Analysis of balances and transactions in individual funds
- Analysis of significant budget variances
- Description of capital assets and long-term debt activity during the period
- Currently known facts, decisions, or conditions expected to affect financial position or results of operations

Government-Wide Financial Statements

Consist of:

- Statement of Net Assets
- Statement of Activities

Report on overall government

- Do not display information about individual funds
- Exclude fiduciary activities or component units that are fiduciary
- Distinction made between primary government and discretely presented component units
- Distinction made between government-type activities and business-type activities of primary government
- Government-type activities include governmental funds & internal service funds
- Business-type activities include enterprise funds only

Characteristics of Government-Wide Financial Statements

Use economic measurement focus for all assets, liabilities, revenues, expenses, gains, & losses

Apply accrual basis of accounting

Revenues from exchanges or exchange-like transactions recognized in period of exchange

Revenues from nonexchange transactions:

- **Derived tax revenues** imposed on exchange transactions recognized as asset & revenues when exchange occurs
- **Imposed nonexchange revenues** imposed on nongovernment agencies recognized as asset when government has enforceable claim & as revenues when use of resources required or permitted
- **Government-mandated nonexchange transactions** provided by one level of government for another recognized as asset & revenue (or liability & expense) when all eligibility requirements met
- **Voluntary nonexchange transactions** recognized similarly to government-mandated nonexchange transactions

Statement of Net Assets

Presents assets & liabilities

- Assets & liabilities in order of liquidity
- Current & noncurrent portions of liabilities reported
- Assets – Liabilities = Net assets

3 categories of net assets

- **Net assets invested in capital assets, net of related debt** – All capital assets, including restricted assets, net of depreciation & reduced by bonds, mortgages, notes, & other borrowings
- **Restricted net assets** – Assets with externally imposed restrictions on use distinguishing major categories of restrictions
- **Unrestricted net assets** – Remainder

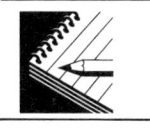

Format of Statement of Net Assets

Assets, liabilities, & net assets reported for primary government

- Separate columns for government-type activities & business-type activities
- Amounts combined in total column

Assets, liabilities, & net assets also reported for component units

- Amounts reported similarly as those for primary government
- Column is **not** combined with totals for primary government

Statement of Activities

Self-financing activities distinguished from those drawing from general revenues

For each government function
- Net expense or revenue
- Relative burden

Governmental activities presented by function

Business-type activities presented by business segment

Items reported separately after net expenses of government's functions:
- General revenues
- Contributions to term & permanent endowments
- Contributions to permanent fund principal
- Special items – those that are unusual **or** infrequent
- Extraordinary items – those that are unusual **and** infrequent
- Transfers

Items on Statement of Activities

Depreciation – indirect expense charged to function with asset

- Allocated among functions for shared assets
- Not required to be allocated to functions for general capital assets
- Not allocated to functions for general infrastructure assets

Revenues classified into categories

- Amounts received from users or beneficiaries of a program always **program revenues**
- Amounts received from parties outside citizenry are **general revenues** if unrestricted or program revenues if restricted to specific programs
- Amounts received from taxpayers always general revenues
- Amounts generated by the government usually general revenues
- Contributions to term & permanent endowments, contributions to permanent fund principal, special & extraordinary items, & transfers reported separately

Format of Statement of Activities

Information for each program or function reported separately:

- Expenses
- Charges for services
- Operating grants & contributions
- Capital grants & contributions

Difference between expenses & revenues reported for each program

- Equal to change in net assets
- Separated into columns for governmental activities and business-type activities
- Combined into a total column

Remaining items (general revenues, grants & contributions, special & extraordinary items, & transfers) reported separately below functions & programs

- Divided into governmental activities & business-type activities with total column
- Provides change in net assets & ending net assets with same amounts as Statement of Net Assets
- Separate column for component units not combined into total

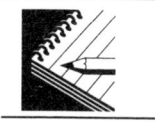

Additional Characteristics of Government-Wide Financial Statements

Internal Amounts

- Eliminated to avoid doubling up
- Interfund receivables & payables eliminated
- Amounts due between government-type & business-type activities presented as offsetting internal balances

Capital assets include the following:

- Land, land improvements, & easements
- Buildings & building improvements
- Vehicles, machinery, & equipment
- Works of art & historical treasures
- Infrastructure
- All other tangible & intangible assets with initial useful lives > a single period

Accounting for Capital Assets & Infrastructure

Capital assets reported at historical cost

- Includes capitalized interest & costs of getting asset ready for intended use
- Depreciated over useful lives
- Inexhaustible assets not depreciated
- Infrastructure assets may be depreciated under modified approach

Infrastructure includes:

- Capital assets with longer lives than most capital assets that are normally stationary
- Roads, bridges, tunnels, drainage systems, water & sewer systems, dams, & lighting systems

Eligible infrastructure assets not depreciated

- Must be part of network or subsystem maintained & preserved at established condition levels
- Additions & improvements increasing capacity or efficiency capitalized
- Other expenditures expensed

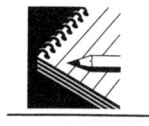

Fund Financial Statements

Governmental funds include:
- General fund
- Special revenue funds
- Capital projects funds
- Debt service funds
- Permanent funds

Proprietary funds include:
- Enterprise funds
- Internal service funds

Fiduciary funds include:
- Pension & other employee benefit trust funds
- Investment trust funds
- Private purpose trust funds
- Agency funds

Financial Statements of Governmental Funds

Statements of governmental funds

- Balance sheet
- Statement of revenues, expenditures, and changes in fund balances

Focus is to report sources, uses, & balances of current financial resources

- Apply modified accrual accounting
- Capital assets & long-term debt not reported as assets or liabilities

Reports include separate columns for each major governmental fund and single column for total of all nonmajor funds:

- General fund is always major
- Others major if assets, liabilities, revenues, expenditures meet the 5% and 10% tests:
  - Fund at least 5% of "total" column in government-wide financial statements
  - Fund at least 10% of "government-type" column in government-wide financial statements.

Balance Sheet

Reports assets, liabilities, & fund balances

- Reported separately for each major governmental fund
- Fund balances segregated into reserved & unreserved

Total fund balances reconciled to net assets of governmental activities in government-wide financial statements

Statement of Revenues, Expenditures, & Changes in Fund Balances

Reports inflows, outflows, and balances of current financial resources

- Reported separately for each major governmental fund
- Revenues classified by major source
- Expenditures classified by function

Format of statement:

Revenues

− Expenditures

= Excess (deficiency) of revenues over expenditures

± Other financing sources and uses

± Special and extraordinary items

= Net change in fund balances

+ Fund balances – beginning of period

= Fund balances – end of period

Change in fund balances reconciled to change in net assets of governmental activities in government-wide financial statements

Financial Statements of Proprietary Funds

Statements of proprietary funds

- Statement of net assets
- Statement of Revenues, Expenses, and Changes in Fund Net Assets
- Statement of Cash Flows

Preparation of statements

- Emphasis is measurement of economic resources
- Prepared under accrual basis of accounting
- Reports include separate column for each enterprise fund meeting 5% and 10% tests:
  - Fund at least 5% of "total" column in government-wide financial statements
  - Fund at least 10% of "business-type" column in government-wide financial statements.
  - Total of non-major enterprise funds in a single column
  - Total of all internal service funds in a single column

Statement of Net Assets

Prepared in classified format

- Current & noncurrent assets & liabilities distinguished
- Net assets reported in same categories as used in government-wide financial statements

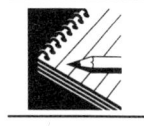

Statement of Revenues, Expenses, & Changes in Fund Net Assets

Amounts should be the same as net assets & changes in net assets shown for business-type activities in government-wide financial statements

- Revenues reported by major source
- Operating & nonoperating revenues & expenses distinguished
- Nonoperating revenues & expenses reported after operating income

Format of statement of revenues, expenses, & changes in fund net assets

	Operating revenues (listed by source)
−	Operating expenses (listed by category)
=	Operating income or loss
±	Nonoperating revenues & expenses
=	Income before other revenues, expenses, gains, losses, & transfers
±	Capital contributions, additions to permanent & term endowments, special & extraordinary items, & transfers
=	Increase or decrease in net assets
+	Net assets – beginning of period
=	Net assets – end of period

Statement of Cash Flows

Shows sources & uses of cash by major classification

- Operating activities reported using direct method
- Noncapital financing activities
- Capital & related financing activities
- Investing activities

Operating income reconciled to cash flows from operating activities (indirect method)

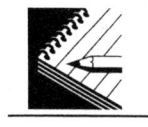

Financial Statements of Fiduciary Funds

Statements of fiduciary funds

- Statement of Net Assets
- Statement of Changes in Fiduciary Net Assets

Focus of fiduciary financial statements

- Emphasis on measurement of economic resources
- Prepared using accrual basis of accounting

Report includes separate column for each major fiduciary fund and column for total of all non-major fiduciary funds.

- Selection of major funds based on judgment of entity management
- No 5% and 10% tests since fiduciary funds weren't included in government-wide financial statements

Notes to Government Financial Statements

Intended to provide information needed for fair presentation of financial statements

Notes will include:

- Summary of significant accounting policies
- Disclosure about capital assets & long-term liabilities
- Disclosure about major classes of capital assets
- Disclosure about donor-restricted endowments
- Segment information

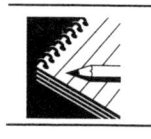

Required Supplementary Information

Presented in addition to MD & A

Consists of:

- Schedule of Funding Progress for all Pension Trust Funds
- Schedule of Employer Contributions to all Pension Trust Funds
- Budgetary comparison schedules for governmental funds (reporting basis is same as that chosen by legislative body for budget, and not necessarily that used for financial statements)
- Information about infrastructure reported under the modified approach
- Claims development information for any public entity risk pools

Governmental Funds

A governmental unit maintains 5 types of governmental funds

- General fund – all activities not accounted for in another fund
- Special revenue funds – account for revenues earmarked to finance specific activities
- Capital projects funds – account for construction of fixed assets
- Debt service fund – accumulates resources for payment of general obligation debts of other governmental funds
- Permanent funds – account for resources that are legally restricted

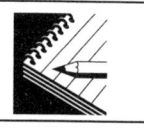

General Fund Accounting

A governmental unit will have one general fund

- Annual budget is recorded at the beginning of the year
- Revenues, expenditure, & other financing sources & uses are recorded during the year
- Adjustments are made at the balance sheet date
- Budgetary accounts are closed at year-end

Beginning of Year

Governmental unit adopts annual budget for general fund

Budget recorded with following entry:

Estimated revenues control	xxx		
Estimated other financing sources	xxx		
Budgetary fund balance	xxx	or	xxx
Appropriations			xxx
Estimated other financing uses			xxx

Estimated revenues control = revenues expected to be collected during the year

Estimated other financing sources = estimate of proceeds from bond issues & operating transfers in

Budgetary fund balance = plug – amount required to balance the entry

Appropriations = expenditures expected during the year

Estimated other financing uses = expected operating transfers out

During the Year

Revenue cycle consists of billing certain revenues, such as property taxes, collecting billed revenues, writing off uncollectible billings, & collecting unbilled revenues

Billing of revenues:

Taxes receivable	xxx	
Allowance for estimated uncollectible taxes		xxx
Deferred revenues		xxx
Revenues control		xxx

Taxes receivable = amount billed

Allowance for estimated uncollectible taxes = billings expected to be uncollectible
- This amount may be adjusted upward or downward during the year
- Offsetting entry will be to revenues control

Deferred revenues = portion of billed taxes expected to be collected more than 60 days after close of current year

Revenues control = portion of billed taxes expected to be collected during the current year or within 60 days of close

During the Year (continued)

Collecting billed revenues:

Cash	xxx	
Taxes receivable		xxx

Writing off uncollectible amounts:

Allowance for estimated uncollectible taxes	xxx	
Taxes receivable		xxx

Collecting unbilled revenues:

Cash	xxx	
Revenues control		xxx

During the Year (continued)

Spending cycle consists of ordering goods & services, receiving the goods & services, and paying for them

Ordering goods & services:

Encumbrances control (estimated cost)	xxx	
Budgetary fund balance reserved for encumbrances		xxx

Receiving goods & services:

Budgetary fund balance reserved for encumbrances (estimated cost)	xxx	
Encumbrances control		xxx
Expenditures control (actual cost)	xxx	
Vouchers payable		xxx

Payment:

Vouchers payable	xxx	
Cash		xxx

During the Year (continued)

Other financing sources & uses are recorded as the transactions occur:

- Proceeds of long-term debit issues are recorded as other financing sources when received

- Operating transfers to or from other funds are reported as other financing uses or sources as the funds are transferred

Adjustments at Balance Sheet Date

Closing entry – eliminating revenues, expenditures, & encumbrances:

Revenues control	xxx		
Unreserved fund balance (plug)	xxx	or	xxx
Expenditures control			xxx
Encumbrances control			xxx

The remaining balance in the budgetary fund balance reserved for encumbrances is transferred to a nonbudgetary account:

Budgetary fund balance reserved for encumbrances	xxx	
Fund balance reserved for encumbrances		xxx

The governmental unit may decide to recognize inventory as an asset:

Inventories (increase)	xxx	
Fund balance reserved for inventories		xxx

or

Fund balance reserved for inventories	xxx	
Inventories (decrease)		xxx

End of Year

Budget recorded in beginning of year is reversed:

Appropriations	xxx		
Estimated other financing uses	xxx		
Budgetary fund balance	xxx	or	xxx
Estimated revenues control			xxx
Estimated other financing sources			xxx

Special Revenue Fund

Used to account for revenues that must be used for a particular purpose

- Accounting identical to general fund

Capital Projects Fund

Used to account for construction of fixed assets

- Fund opened when project commences & closed when project complete
- Accounting similar to general fund

Differences in accounting for capital projects fund:

1) Budgetary entries generally not made
2) Expenditures generally made under contract
   - Credit contracts payable
   - Credit retention payable for deferred payments

Debt Service Fund

Used to account for funds accumulated to make principal & interest payments on general obligation debts

- Expenditures include principal & interest payable in current period
- Resources consist of amounts transferred from other funds (other financing sources) & earnings on investments (revenues)

Amounts used for interest payments separated from amounts used for principal payments

Cash for interest	xxx	
Cash for principal	xxx	
Other financing sources		xxx

Proprietary Funds

Account for governmental activities conducted similarly to business enterprises

Enterprise fund:

- Used to account for business-type activities
- Uses accrual basis accounting
- Earned income recognized as operating revenues
- Shared taxes reported as nonoperating revenues

Internal service fund:

- Used to account for services provided to other governmental departments on a fee or cost-reimbursement basis
- Resources come from billings to other funds
- Reported as operating revenues

Fiduciary Funds

Pension Trust Fund

Accounts for contributions made by government & employees using accrual accounting

Additional information in notes and supplementary information following notes will include:

- Description of plan and classes of employees covered
- Summary of significant accounting policies
- Information about contributions including description of how contributions are determined and required contribution rates of plan members
- Information about legally required reserves at reporting date

Investment Trust Fund

Accounts for assets received from other governments units to be invested on their behalf.

- Uses accrual accounting

Private Purpose Trust Fund

Accounts for resources held on behalf of private persons or organizations.

- Uses accrual accounting

Agency Fund

Accounts for money collected for various funds, other governments, or outsiders

- Includes only balance sheet accounts
- Assets always equal liabilities
- Uses modified accrual accounting

Interfund Transactions

Nonreciprocal transfers are transfers of resources from one fund to another without any receipts of goods or services, such as a transfer of money from the general fund to a capital projects fund

Paying fund:

Other financing uses control	xxx	
Cash		xxx

Receiving fund:

Cash	xxx	
Other financing sources control		xxx

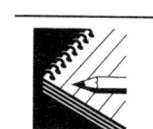

Interfund Transactions (continued)

Reciprocal transfers occur when one fund acquires goods or services from another in a transaction similar to one that would occur with outsiders

Paying fund:
    Expenditures control **or** Expenses   xxx
        Cash   xxx

Receiving fund:
    Cash   xxx
        Revenues control   xxx

Reimbursements occur when one fund makes payments on behalf of another fund

Reimbursing fund:
    Expenditures control **or** Expenses   xxx
        Cash   xxx

Receiving fund:
    Cash   xxx
        Expenditures control **or** Expenses   xxx

Interfund Transactions (continued)

Loans may be made one fund to another

Lending fund:
    Due from other fund (fund identified)   xxx
        Cash   xxx

Receiving fund:
    Cash   xxx
        Due to other fund (fund identified)   xxx

Solid Waste Landfill Operations

Environmental Protection Agency imposes requirements on solid waste landfills

- Procedures for closures
- Procedures for postclosure care

Procedures represent long-term obligations accounted for as long-term debt

- Costs to be incurred by governmental funds accounted for in general long-term debt account group
- Expenditures in governmental funds reduce general long-term debt account group balances
- Costs to be incurred by proprietary funds accounted for directly in funds
- Costs associated with closure and postclosure procedures accounted for during periods of operation

Accounting for Nonprofit Entities

Financial Statements of Not-for-Profit Organizations

All not-for-profit organizations must prepare at least 3 financial statements

Not-for-profit organizations include:
- Hospitals
- Colleges & universities
- Voluntary health & welfare organizations (VHW)

Required financial statements for all types include:
- Statement of Financial Position
- Statement of Activities
- Statement of Cash Flows

VHWs must also prepare a Statement of Functional Expenses

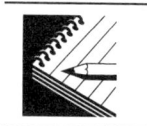

Statement of Financial Position

Includes assets, liabilities, & net assets

- Unrestricted net assets – available for general use, including those set aside by board of trustees
- Temporarily restricted net assets – donated by outside party & restricted to specific purpose
- Permanently restricted net assets – donated by outside party & required to be invested with earnings restricted or unrestricted

Not-for-Profit Company
Statement of Financial Position
December 31, 20X2

Assets:		Liabilities:	
Cash	100	Accounts payable	50
Marketable securities	300	Notes payable	100
Accounts receivable, net	40	Bonds payable	100
Inventory	120	Total liabilities	250
P, P, & E	80	Net assets:	
Total assets	640	Unrestricted	45
		Temporarily restricted	305
		Permanently restricted	40
		Total net assets	390
		Total liabilities & net assets	640

Statement of Activities for NPO

Similar to income statement

- Reports revenues, gains, expenses, & losses
- Also reports temporarily restricted assets released from restriction
- Categorized activities among unrestricted, temporarily restricted, & permanently restricted to provide change in net assets for each
- Change added to beginning balance to provide ending net assets for each category

Expenses classified by:

- Object – nature of item or service obtained
- Function – program or activity to which attributed
- Character – period or periods benefited from payments

Statement of Activities *(continued)*

	Total	Unrestricted	Temporarily Restricted	Permanently Restricted
Revenues & gains				
Donations	665	265	360	40
Investment income	10	10		
Total revenues & gains	675	275	360	40
Net assets released from restriction				
Research restrictions		100	(100)	
Time restrictions				
Property restrictions		20	(20)	
Total net assets released from restriction		120	(120)	
Expenses & losses				
Depreciation	(10)	(10)		
Program expenses	(190)	(190)		
General & administrative	(85)	(85)		
Salaries	(70)	(70)		
Total expenses & losses	(355)	(355)		
Change in net assets	320	40	240	40
Net assets at December 31, 20X1	70	5	65	
Net assets at December 31, 20X2	390	45	305	40

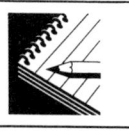

Statement of Cash Flows for NPO

Similar to statement of cash flows under GAAP

- Special treatment for donated assets restricted for long-term purposes
- Classified as cash flows from financing activities

Statement of Functional Expenses

Classifies expenses into program services & support services

- Program services – expenses directly related to organization's purpose
- Support services – expenses necessary, but not directly related to organization's purpose such as fund-raising & administrative expenses

Expenses classified by (similar to statement of activities):

- Object
- Nature
- Character

Contributions Made to and Received by Not-for-Profit Organizations

In general, contributions are income to a not-for-profit organization

- Those that are part of the major, ongoing, & central operations are revenues
- Those that are not are gains

Unrestricted cash donations:

Cash	xxx	
Donations (unrestricted funds)		xxx

Permanently restricted donations:

Cash	xxx	
Donations (permanently restricted funds)		xxx

Donated services:

Program expense (fair market value)	xxx	
Donations (unrestricted funds)		xxx

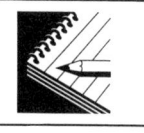

Contributions Made to and Received by Not-for-Profit Organizations (continued)

Cash donations restricted for a specific purposes:

When made:

Cash	xxx	
Donations (temporarily restricted funds)		xxx

When used:

Temporarily restricted net assets	xxx	
Unrestricted net assets		xxx
Expense	xxx	
Cash		xxx

Cash donated for purchase of property:

When made:

Cash	xxx	
Donations (temporarily restricted funds)		xxx

When used:

Temporarily restricted net assets	xxx	
Unrestricted net assets		xxx
Property	xxx	
Cash		xxx

Pledges

Promises by outside parties to donate assets

- Recognized in period of pledge
- Allowance for uncollectible amount established
- Some or all may have time restriction – temporarily restricted
- Some or all may be unrestricted

Pledges	xxx	
Allowance for uncollectible pledges		xxx
Donations (unrestricted funds)		xxx
Donations (temporarily restricted funds)		xxx

Other Donations

Donations of art, antiques, or artifacts not recognized if:

- Asset held for research or exhibition
- Asset preserved & unaltered
- Proceeds from sale of asset to be used to buy additional art, antiques, & artifacts

Donated assets to be held in trust

- Not recognized by not-for-profit organization
- Disclosed in footnotes to financial statements

Hospital Revenues

Patient service revenue recorded at gross value of services

- Billing may be less due to Medicare allowance or employee discount
- Difference recorded in allowance account
- Statement of activities will report net amount

Services provided for free due to charity not recognized as revenues

Special transactions:

- Bad debts recognized as expense on statement of activities, not reduction of revenues
- Miscellaneous revenues from cafeteria, gift shop, parking lot fees, & educational programs classified as other revenue
- Donated supplies reported as operating revenue & expense when used
- Donations of essential services and unrestricted donations are nonoperating revenues

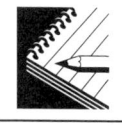

College Tuition Revenues

Students may receive refunds or price breaks

Refunds to students reduce tuition revenues

Price breaks may result from scholarships or reductions for family members of faculty or staff

- Tuition recognized at gross amount
- Price break recognized as expense

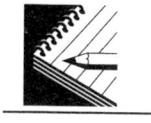